Jesus Concealed
in
the Old Testament

The Preincarnate Christ
by Pastor Paul Wallace

Published by Paul Wallace
Sedona, Arizona

Copyrighted © 2005; 2nd Edition 2008
Paul Wallace
All Rights reserved.
ISBN#1-59196-903-4
Printed in the USA by Instantpublishing.com

Unless otherwise noted, Scripture quotations are taken from the *Holy Bible, New International Version (NIV)* Copyright © 1973, 1978, 1984 by International Bible Society. All rights reserved.
Scripture quotations marked *KJV* are taken from the *King James Version*

Special thanks to Dennis and Karen Richards for their proofreading assistance.

Forward

There have been a number of books written on Jesus in the Old Testament, but for some reason the topic has not been taught in most churches today. Academia usually refers to the topic as typology. When I teach on this subject, the first response is, "Why haven't we heard of this before?" Topics like this make their rounds over the years falling in and out of favor. Because it has been neglected for so long, I've found great excitement each time I have presented it.

The way I have laid out the material requires that you look up the verses. In home study groups, it would be helpful to assign each passage to a different person to help the study flow more smoothly. I encourage you to add things that you discover, as you surely will. This is by no means an exhaustive study on the subject. I have not included the many prophecies of the coming Messiah. That is a study in itself.

My hope is that you will see the sovereignty of God in all of history and His great desire to reveal His Son.

Contents

Jesus in Genesis
- Theophanies — 5
- Prophecy — 12
- Types and Shadows — 17
- Types and Shadows 2 — 24

Exodus
- Part One — 29
- The Feasts of Israel — 34
- The Tabernacle — 53

Leviticus — 58
Numbers — 64
Deuteronomy — 69

The Old Testament — 74
Conclusion — 80

Jesus in Genesis
Theophanies

Jesus' name does not appear in Genesis. Jesus of Nazareth would not be born for thousands of years, so why look for Him here? It has been said that the Old Testament is the New Testament concealed, and the New Testament is the Old Testament revealed. Since the New Testament is all about Jesus, we should certainly find Him concealed in the Old Testament.

New Testament authors and Jesus Himself point us to look for Him in the Old Testament. Jesus said, *Abraham rejoiced at the thought of seeing my day; he saw it and was glad.* And *Before Abraham was born, I am.* John 8:56,58b *Moses wrote of me* John 5:46. And then there was that personal Bible study by Jesus with the two on the road to Emmaus. *And beginning with Moses and all the Prophets, he explained to them what was said in **all** the Scriptures concerning himself.* (Luke 24:27) (bold mine)

The two disciples on the road to Emmaus were downcast because of Jesus' death. Before Jesus showed them He was alive and speaking with them, He wanted them to see God was working out a plan that had not changed. He was showing them the sovereignty of an all-powerful God. In seeing that, they came to a faith in the greatness of God that overcame their fears and concerns. Jesus showed the other disciples the same wonderful truth. *He said to them, "This is what I told you while I was still with you: Everything must be fulfilled that is written about me in the Law of Moses, the Prophets and the Psalms."* (Luke 24:44) It's all about Jesus!

The main message of the Apostles was that Jesus had risen from the dead, but equal to that was the teaching that He is the fulfillment of the writings of Moses and the prophets. They took what Jesus had revealed to them and used it as a witnessing tool for the salvation of the Jews who had ears to hear. If they used it as a witnessing tool, shouldn't we at least understand some of what they surely taught as they passed on the teaching they received from Jesus? Take a moment to look at how frequently they referred to this topic as they shared the Gospel. (Acts 3:18,24, 10:43, 15:15-18, 24:14, 26:22-23, 28:23)

The rabbis often refer to Genesis as "The Book of Creation". With that in mind, read the words of the Apostle Paul in Colossians 1:15-18 *He is the image of the invisible God, the firstborn over all creation. For by him all things were created: things in heaven and on earth, visible and invisible, whether thrones of powers or rulers or authorities; all things were created by him and for him. He is before all things, and in him all things hold together. And he is the head of the body, the church; he is the beginning and the firstborn from among the dead, so that in everything he might have the supremacy.*

How could the "Book of Creation" not be filled with Jesus when He is the instrument of creation and the reason for creation? If all things were created for Him, what should that mean to your life? Actually, everything is about Jesus! In this book of beginnings, He has the supremacy.

There are three ways in which we will look at the revelation of Christ in Genesis. The first is His very being. This study will begin with a glimpse of Jesus before His incarnation. The theological term for a preincarnational appearance of Christ is "Theophany" or "Christophany". Not all these references deal with an appearance. Some simply refer to Him. We will begin right in chapter one. This is one of the most debated and disputed chapters of the Bible. Until approximately 30 years ago, the first line was mocked. Scientists were sure there was no creation event, no beginning. Today their tune has changed, as the idea of a beginning moment is gaining wide acceptance. Even in Stephen Hawking's formulas of creation, there is an interesting factor called the outside influence or force. There is no explanation as to what or who the force is. The greatest scientists recognize that the universe is too finely tuned to be a product of mere chance.

Lets look at the Biblical account. Genesis 1:1 *In the beginning God...* God is the Hebrew word Elohim. El is singular for God. The "im" ending makes Hebrew words plural, so we literally have, "In the beginning Gods..." All Jews are familiar with the *shema*, a quote from Deuteronomy 6:4. *Hear O Israel the Lord our God is one.* Here too, Elohim is used. The Lord our Gods are one. So we see a plural proper noun that is in complete unity. It sounds like Jesus' statement in the gospel of John, *I and my Father are one.* (John 10:30 KJV)

Is Jesus the Christ at work in creation? We read Colossians 1:16 that claims it was by Him (Jesus) that all things were created. 1 Corinthians 8:6 tells us that all things came from God, but it adds they came through Jesus Christ. Hebrews 1:2, 10-12 also tells that it is through Jesus that the universe was made. Psalm 102:24-27 refers to Elohim as the One whose hands made the universe. The only way to understand these verses together is to know that Jesus was speaking the truth when He claimed to be one with the Father. Proverbs 30:4 is an interesting reference to the

Creator and his Son. *Who has gone up to heaven and come down? Who has gathered up the wind in the hollow of his hands? Who has wrapped up the waters in his cloak? Who has established all the ends of the earth? What is his name, and the name of his son? Tell me if you know!*

Now, understanding that John 1:14 teaches us that Jesus is the Word of God made flesh; look at Genesis 1:3. *And God said...* God is the One from whom the words come, and those words are Jesus. The words through Whom creation comes into existence are Jesus, the Word of God. Each time you read of God speaking, you are reading of Jesus. *Through faith we understand that the worlds were framed by the word of God, so that things which are seen were not made of things which do appear.* (Hebrews 11:3 KJV)

The Targums, (explanatory versions of the Old Testament in Aramaic by expositors of the Torah) refer to the Word as *Mimra* and out of the 596 usages, half are personified.*

We are going to save the many revelations of Jesus in types and prophecy for later studies and jump to the next direct reference to Jesus. Genesis 1:26a (KJV), *And God said, Let us make man in our image, after our likeness:* Who is the *us*? He's the same that we have already been referring to as the instrument of creation. The Father uttered the Word and matter came into being.

And they heard the voice of the LORD God walking in the garden in the cool of the day: and Adam and his wife hid themselves from the presence of the LORD God amongst the trees of the garden. Genesis 3:8 (KJV) Who walked with Adam and Eve in the Garden? God the Father is a spirit. (John 4:24) Only Christ (the voice of the Lord) takes on a form. (Hebrews 10:5; Colossians 1:15; John 14:9) Compare Genesis 4:26 with Acts 4:10-12.

And Melchizedek king of Salem brought forth bread and wine: and he was the priest of the most high God. (Genesis 14:18 KJV) Melchizedek is, in my opinion, a theophany. He is the King of Salem (peace). See Hebrews 7:1-4. Jesus is referred to as the Prince of peace. Melchizedek served communion to Abraham, the father of faith. He is a priest of God Most High and the author of Hebrews calls Jesus our great High Priest. He blesses Abraham and without exception the lesser is blessed by the greater.

There are many scholars who do not reach the same conclusion, but I do not see how it could be anyone but Christ. If he is a mere man, how could Christ be a priest after his order? Would that not make Christ's authority only an earthly one? The founder of the order is greater than those who come after him in almost every case. If He is King of Righteousness and Peace and yet was not Jesus, would that not make him greater than Jesus the Prince of Peace?

This also helps us understand why the judgment on the Canaanites in the days of Joshua was so severe. The Canaanites had the witness of Melchizedek and Abraham and yet fell into perverse religious practices.

You are certainly welcome to disagree with my conclusion, as this is a debated Theophany. But to say he is not Jesus raises many more questions.

Next we have the three strange guests that come to visit Abraham and to inspect Sodom and Gomorrah in Genesis 18.

¹ And the LORD appeared unto him in the plains of Mamre: and he sat in the tent door in the heat of the day; ² And he lift up his eyes and looked, and, lo, three men stood by him: and when he saw them, he ran to meet them from the tent door, and bowed himself toward the ground, (Genesis 18:1-2 KJV)

Notice the first verse says the LORD appeared to Abraham. When you see all capital spelling of LORD it is a translation of the Hebrew word Jehovah. This is the solemn holy name for God that a Hebrew could not utter aloud. In writing the name the vowels are dropped. JHWH – when written on vellum, the custom is to write it in gold so that it will not accidentally be pronounced.

Who are these other two 'men'? Perhaps they are the angels of the next chapter. See Genesis 19:1. Abraham had a conversation with this Theophany who looked like a man yet he acknowledges Him to be Jehovah. They discussed judgment of the city and the number of righteous people that would be required to save it. The Son is the One who is given authority to judge. (John 5:27)

What lessons can we learn with Abraham's discussion with Jesus? See Genesis 18:14,15 and 20-33. Abraham saw both Melchizedek and this appearance of Jehovah. I wonder if they looked the same or were different manifestations?

Isaac visually saw the LORD in Genesis 26:24, and the covenant was renewed with him. *And the LORD appeared unto him the same night, and said, I am the God of Abraham thy father: fear not, for I am with thee, and will bless thee, and multiply thy seed for my servant Abraham's sake.* (Genesis 26:24 KJV)

Jesus in the Old Testament

Jacob saw the LORD in a dream, and the covenant was renewed to him as well. See Genesis 28:13-17. Verse 21b is interesting. *...then shall the LORD be my God,* (Genesis 28:21b KJV) or literally Jehovah will be my Elohim.

In Genesis 32:24 –30, Jacob wrestled with a Theophany. Not something I would want to try. In verse 30, he calls the man, "God". Notice the 'el' on the end of Peniel. The Rabbis say that this "angel of his presence" means the "Angel of the Covenant and the Prince of the Countenance". In Hebrew, the phrase Sar ha-Panim, literally means "the Prince of faces" or "countenance". The Jewish prayer book, the *Sidur ha-Shalem,* contains the New Year prayers in connection with the sounding of the *shofar* horn. There is a remarkable prayer that speaks of "Jesus the Prince of the Countenance". The prayer also refers to Jesus as the *Metatron* meaning the One who sits on the throne.* Even the Jewish New Year prayers declare Jesus to be the One that appeared in Genesis!

Do you ever wrestle in some sense with Jesus?
In what way? Did Jacob win or lose the wrestling match?

What does it mean to you to see that Jesus appears in the book of Genesis?

For more direct references to Jesus see
Genesis 16:6-16; 22:9-18. Next we will look at the prophecies concerning Jesus. Then we will cover the types and shadows in the following chapters.

* Risto Santala, *The Messiah in the Old Testament in the Light of Rabbinical Writings,* p 89
*Ibid p 86

Jesus in Genesis
Prophecy

In the last chapter, we looked at direct references to Jesus in Genesis. In this chapter, we will examine some of the prophecies concerning Jesus the Messiah. There are many prophetic types that we will look at in the following chapters, but this study is limited to those prophecies that are directly referring to the Messiah.

The first is found in chapter three verse fifteen. This passage is known as *the proto-evangel*. Although the New Testament does not quote this passage, some believe Romans 16:20 alludes to it. The early church father, Iranaeus, refers to it in the second century and may have been taught this by his mentor Polycarp, John the Beloved's disciple.

And I will put enmity between you and the woman, and between your offspring (seed) and hers; he will crush your head, and you will bruise his heel." (Genesis 3:15) The Lord is speaking to the Serpent. Enmity can be translated hatred. Because Satan had seduced Eve into taking the forbidden fruit, causing spiritual death, God pronounced this sentence upon Satan. His seed and the seed of woman would have hatred between them. The seed of the woman would crush the serpent's head, while the serpent would bruise His heel.

Let's examine each piece of this forecast given by the Lord. *I will put hatred between you and the woman, and between your seed and hers...* God has placed hatred between the sons of Satan and Christ. I have used sons of Satan in place of 'your seed'. (John 8:44) In the place of 'hers' – meaning her seed, I have put Christ. John 7:7 states, *The world cannot hate you, but it hates me because I testify that what it does is evil.* Children of the world hate Christ. To them He represents a loss of freedom and pleasure. What does the Truth really bring to our lives? (John 8:32)

...he will crush your head... The seed of the woman, Jesus, will crush the head (authority, rule) of Satan. There is a picture here, of a man's heel on the head of a snake, grinding it into the ground. Satan's seduction of Eve that resulted in disobedience to God brought about the curse of death. This was Satan's plan, because his goal is to kill, steal and destroy. (John 10:10) Jesus, on the other hand, came to bring life, and so He had to break the power of the curse on mankind. (Hebrew 2:9-14)

Mankind lost the right to life when they disobeyed God. We think of life as having a heartbeat. The Word teaches us that life is communion with God. (John 17:3) How could man regain the life he had lost through sin? A man had to regain that right, but none were able. Man had the authority and title as Prince of the World, but there in the Garden, he gave it up to Satan. Man had to take the right to the title back, but man was unable. So God clothed Himself in flesh, becoming the God-man, Jesus, to take back the right to the Tree of Life. He took the curse of sin, which is death, upon Himself. The thorns He wore on His head, as He became a curse for us by hanging on a tree (the cross), are a picture of Him bearing the curse. The Just took the punishment for the unjust. Because He did this for us, God the Father gave His only Son a place above all. (Philippians 2:6-11, Colossians 2:13-15) That completed, God could justly give life (fellowship with God) to all who come to Him by faith.

...and you will bruise his heel. It was not without cost that the Christ was able to redeem us. It came at great personal sacrifice. *They pierced my hands and my feet.* (Psalm 22:16b) "He" in the prophecy was to crush the head of Satan and be wounded in the heel by him. This is the first direct prophecy of the coming of a Deliverer who would save us from the Deceiver.

The next prophecy has an affirmation in the New Testament. *In thy Seed shall all the nations of the earth be blessed* (Genesis 22:18 KJV) Genesis 12:3, 17:7, 21:12, 26:4, 28:14 find New Testament fulfillment in Galatians 3:16 (KJV). *Now to Abraham and his seed were the promises made. He saith not, And to seeds, as of many; but as of one, And to thy seed, which is Christ.*

The Apostle Paul was very specific in pointing out that these promises of blessing for the earth were not in the descendants of Abraham but in a descendant. This is the same Seed of the woman that would crush the head of Satan. This is the way He would bless the nations of the earth, by crushing the authority of the one who seeks to kill, steal and destroy.

Next, Genesis 49:8-12 records the blessing of Jacob to his son Judah. Jesus descended from this line.

[8]Judah, thou art he whom thy brethren shall praise: thy hand shall be in the neck of thine enemies; thy father's children shall bow down before thee. [9] Judah is a lion's whelp: from the prey, my son, thou art gone up: he stooped down, he couched as a lion, and as an old lion; who shall rouse him up? [10]The sceptre shall not depart from Judah, nor a lawgiver from between his feet, until Shiloh come; and

unto him shall the gathering of the people be. *¹¹Binding his foal unto the vine, and his ass's colt unto the choice vine; he washed his garments in wine, and his clothes in the blood of grapes: ¹²His eyes shall be red with wine, and his teeth white with milk.* (Genesis 49:8-12 KJV)

Notice what is promised: brother's praise, hand on the neck of his enemy, brothers' worship, like a lion, ruling, until Shiloh comes (He to whom it belongs). We note that all of these things apply to the Seed of Judah, Jesus, the lion of the tribe of Judah. (Revelation 5:5) He is praised and worshiped by His brothers. Shiloh can also be translated "him to whom tribute is due". The only One worthy of praise, the only One that has the right to rule, the One Who history is for, and to, and through, is Shiloh – Jesus! (Luke 1:32)

It is not only the Christians who see this as a prophecy of the Messiah, but the rabbis of old did also. They placed particular emphasis on ruling, and in Genesis 49:11, tethering his donkey to a vine. The Talmud indicates the vine to be Israel and the donkey is a word very much like 'his city' in Hebrew. The rabbis also equate the donkey with the humility of the Messiah. (Zechariah 9:9)

We have one more prophetic word about Christ from this time period but not in the book of Genesis. We do not have the book from which this prophecy is taken, but we find the half-brother of Jesus, Jude, quoting from it. *¹⁴ And Enoch also, the seventh from Adam, prophesied of these, saying, Behold, the Lord cometh with ten thousands of his saints, ¹⁵ To execute judgment upon all, and to convince all that are ungodly among them of all their ungodly deeds which they have ungodly committed, and of all their hard speeches which ungodly sinners have spoken against him.* (Jude 1:14-15 KJV)

Enoch saw the second coming of the Messiah. What Jude was quoting was probably one of the first prophecies of the Second Coming of Jesus. There, in the time period early in Genesis, Enoch saw Jesus coming to judge the world.

This thread of prophecy throughout the book gave the patriarchs and the nation of Israel their first clues as to what to expect of this coming Messiah. If we put all these together, we have a picture of One, that is a man, who is coming to crush the Serpent's authority but at a cost. He will bless the nations of the earth. He will reign forever in power even though He comes to Israel in humility. He will judge the world. Those were the first glimpses, but together they made a perfect outline of the coming Messiah. The types, which we will look at in the next chapters, fill in many of the details.

What does it mean to you that the coming of Jesus is detailed from the beginning? Do you have the holy hunger – *'more than my necessary food'* - to know Him? *This is life eternal, that they may know Thee, the only true God and Jesus Christ whom Thou hast sent.* (John 17:3 KJV)

Jesus in Genesis
Types and Shadows 1

We've looked briefly at Jesus in direct references and in prophecy. Now we will see Him in the types and shadows in Genesis.

Is everything directed by the hand of God? (Isaiah 46:10) Are the details of lives drawn up before we are conceived? (Psalm 139:16) Could those details be an instrument to help us see the Messiah, to recognize Him? (Galatians 1:15,16) If God chose to reveal his Son in Paul the Apostle, perhaps He chose to reveal him in individuals in Genesis also. (Hebrews 10:1)

Because there are so many types and shadows in Genesis, instead of elaborating on each, I will list many of them with the parallel New Testament verse. You can draw the connections and implications on your own. Some of this material is from *Christ in All the Scriptures* by A. M. Hodgkin. Of course, all the types fall short in some way, but in them you will see parallels to Christ. Please take the time to look up the passages. You will be astounded at all the pictures of Jesus.

<u>Light</u>
OT: Genesis 1:3 The first thing God is said to have spoken into existence.
NT: John 8:12 *I am the Light of the world*. Colossians 1:15 *He is the image of the invisible God, the firstborn over all creation*. Also see Psalm 27:1; 76:4; 104:2

Covering
OT: Genesis 3:21 *The LORD God made garments of skin for Adam and his wife and clothed them.*
NT: To atone is to cover. Just as some animal had to die to cover the nakedness of Adam and Eve so Christ had to die so our sins could be covered
OT: Genesis 8:13, the Ark had a covering. Those under the covering were saved.
NT: Jesus is our covering. In Him we are saved.

Adam
OT: The first natural man – See Romans 5:19. By contrast, we bear the likeness of the earthly man. *…Adam, the Son of God* (Luke 3:38)
NT: 1Corinthians 15:45,49 *The first man Adam became a living being; the last Adam a life giving spirit…*, the first spiritual man. *We bear the likeness of the man from heaven*. John 3:16 (KJV) *…He gave his only begotten son*.
OT: Genesis 2:22 *Then the LORD God made a woman…and he brought her to the man*. Adam's side was wounded to create his bride.
NT: Revelation 21:2 *I saw the Holy City, the New Jerusalem, coming down out of heaven from God, prepared as a bride beautifully dressed for her husband*. Jesus' side was wounded to create His bride. (John 19:34)

The Tree of Life
OT: Genesis 2:9 (KJV) *In the midst of the Garden was the Tree of Life*.
NT: John 14:6 *I am … the life*. Matthew 18:20 *Where two or three are gathered in my name there am I in their midst*.

Abel

OT: He was a shepherd.
NT: John 10 *I am the Good Shepherd*
OT: Genesis 4:4 He offered an acceptable sacrifice.
NT: Hebrews 10:12-14 Jesus offered an acceptable sacrifice, Himself.
OT: Genesis 4:10 His blood cries to God. Hebrews11:4
NT: Hebrews 12:24 So does that of Jesus.

Enoch
OT: Hebrews 11:5 *...commended as one who pleased God*
NT: John 5:30 *...I seek not to please myself but him who sent me.*
OT: ...he could not be found because he was translated
NT: John 7:34 *You will look for me and will not find me...*
OT: Hebrews 11:6 Enoch believed that He rewards those that diligently seek Him.
NT: Hebrews 12:2 *...who for the joy set before him endured the cross, scorning its shame....* Jesus expected God's reward. Will you walk with God, expecting a great reward?
OT: Genesis 5:24 *Enoch walked with God*
NT: Mark 1:35; John 17:4 No one walked closer than Jesus.

The Ark
OT: The ark was the salvation of God.
NT: Jeshua/Jesus = The salvation of Jehovah
OT: The ark was God's plan. It had to be made according to His measure.
NT: Romans 3:24,25 The redemption that is in Christ Jesus is also God's plan.
OT: It was a place of safety.
NT: Hebrews 6:18 *...take hold of the hope offered to us...*
OT: The ark had to be entered by the door.
NT: John 10:9 (KJV) *I am the door, by me if any man enter in He shall be saved....*

OT: The ark bore the storm of judgment.
NT: Psalm 42:7 (KJV) *All Thy waves and Thy billows are gone over me.* Psalm 69:2 (A messianic psalm) ...I am come into the deep waters where the floods overflow Me. (KJV)
OT: All life was in the ark.
NT: Colossians 3:4; John 1:4 *In Him was life.*
OT: The ark carried Noah's family to a new life.
NT: 2Corinthians 5:17 Life in Jesus is a new life.
OT: The story concludes with a covenant guaranteeing freedom from judgment.
NT: 1Corinthians 11:25; Romans 5:9 Jesus said His blood was a new covenant that guaranteed we will not face judgment.

Isaac

OT: Genesis 22:2 (KJV) *Take now thy son...*
NT: 1John 4:14 (KJV) *...the Father has sent his son to be the Savior of the world.*
OT: Genesis 22:2 (KJV) *Thine only son...*
NT: John 3:16 (KJV) *...his only begotten Son*
OT: Genesis 22:2 (KJV) *Whom thou lovest...*
NT: John 1:18 (KJV) *...in the bosom of the Father*
OT: Genesis 22:2 (KJV) *And get thee into the land of Moriah, upon one of the mountains I will tell thee of... And offer him there for a burnt offering.*
NT: Luke 23:33 (KJV) *And when they were come to the place which is called Calvary (on Mount Mariah), there they crucified Him.* Hebrews 10:5-10 Sanctified through the offering of the body of Jesus Christ once for all.
OT: Genesis 22:4 (KJV) *...Abraham lifted up his eyes and saw the place afar off.*
NT: Acts 3:18 (KJV) *...God before had shewed by the mouth of all His prophets what Christ should suffer....*

Jesus in the Old Testament

OT Genesis 22:6 (KJV) *And Abraham took the wood and the burnt offering, and laid it upon Isaac his son… And they went both of them together.*

NT: John 19:17 (KJV) *And He, bearing His cross, went forth….* John 10:17 (KJV) *Therefore doth My Father love Me, because I lay down My life….*

OT: Genesis 22:7 (KJV) *…where is the lamb for a burnt offering?*

NT: John 1:29 (KJV) *…Behold the Lamb of God that taketh away the sin of the world.*

OT: Genesis 22:8 (RV) *…God will provide Himself the lamb…So they went both of them together.* (The Hebrew implies a unity of purpose.)

NT: Revelation 13:8 (KJV) *…The Lamb slain from the foundation of the world.* Psalm 40:8 (KJV) *I delight to do Thy will, O my God…*

OT: Genesis 22:9-10 (KJV) *…Abraham built an altar there,… and bound Isaac his son, and laid him upon the altar upon the wood. And Abraham stretched forth his hand, and took the knife to slay his son.*

NT: Acts 2:23 (KJV) *Him being delivered by the determinate counsel and foreknowledge of God….* Also Isaiah 53:6 (KJV) *…The Lord hath laid on Him the iniquity of us all.* Isaiah 53:10 *It was the LORD's will to crush him…*

OT: Genesis 22:11 (KJV) *The angel of the LORD called unto him out of heaven…*

NT: Matthew 27:46 (KJV)…*My God, My God why hast Thou forsaken me?* Contrast (no voice from heaven)

OT: Genesis 22:12 (KJV) *…Thou hast not withheld thy son, thine only son….*

NT: Matthew 27:42 (KJV) *He saved others, Himself He cannot save….* Jeremiah 6:26 (When God speaks of deep grief He compares it to the loss of an only son.)

OT: Genesis 22:13 Abraham took the ram, and offered him up for a burnt offering instead of his son.
NT: Isaiah prophesied of the New Testament fulfillment in Isaiah 53:7,11 (KJV) ...*He is brought as a lamb to the slaughter...He shall bear their iniquities.*
OT: Abraham and Jesus both believed that God could resurrect life, Genesis 22:5 Abraham said they would return. See Hebrews 11:19
NT: Jesus told the disciples many times that on the third day He would rise from the dead.

We don't see Isaac again until he comes to meet his bride. From both sacrifices on Moriah until they welcome their bride, Christ and Isaac are strangely absent.

After they worshipped by sacrificing the ram God provided, the angel of the Lord reiterated the promise of blessing the world through Abraham's seed. The amazing thing is that the blessing would take place on that very spot. That was where Jesus died for our sins so that we might become children of God.

The end of the chapter introduces the future wife of Isaac, Rebecca. In a parallel perspective, the sacrifice of Jesus introduces us to his bride, the church. What an incredible picture was painted for us of the Messiah in the life of Isaac.

<u>Wife of Isaac</u>
OT: Genesis 24:7 The servant goes to seek a wife for Isaac with assistance of angels.
NT: Hebrews 1:14 The Holy Spirit seeks the bride of Christ with angelic assistance.
OT: Genesis 24:16 The bride is beautiful.

Jesus in the Old Testament

NT: So are you in God's eyes! 2Corinthians 11:2; Revelations 19:7-8,21:2; Song of Songs 1:5
OT: Genesis 24:22. The servant gives gifts to the bride
NT: 1Corinthians 12 The Holy Spirit gives gifts to the bride.
OT: Genesis 24:36. Isaac is the heir of all.
NT: John 17:10 Jesus is heir of all.
OT: Genesis 24:58. She chose to follow, leaving her family.
NT: Matthew 4:20, 19:27 *We left everything to follow You!*
OT: Genesis 25:22-23 *The babies jostled each other within her…Two nations are in your womb….*
NT: Galatians 5:17 *For the sinful nature desires what is contrary to the Spirit, and the Spirit what is contrary to the sinful nature. They are in conflict with each other….*

What is the Spirit speaking to you as you consider these parallels?

Why would God paint so many portraits of Christ in Genesis?

Does Colossians 2:2,3 have any connection with this study?

Do you feel you may understand a little more how the two on the road to Emmaus were in awe as Christ opened the Scriptures about Himself?

Jesus in Genesis
Types and Shadows 2

As we continue with our study of the portraits of Christ in the book of beginnings, there can be a tendency to just stay on the academic level...but I would encourage you to see Jesus. As God so faithfully and lovingly painted picture after picture of His only begotten Son, take time to look at each portrait and consider what He means to you personally. The angels adore Him. God is pleased with Him; the departed saints sing their praise falling down before Him. What a mighty God we serve! What is your perception of Him?

The last chapter looked at Isaac as a type. His son, Jacob, had two wives that are a type of Israel and the church. Rachael was sought after (like Israel) but Leah became the actual first wife and fruitful (the church). It was later that the marriage with Rachael was consummated and fruitful. Is this a shadow of the day when all Israel shall be saved? Romans 11:26

To get the most out of this study, take time to look up each verse. Understand how each of these pictures foreshadows Christ.

Jacob's Ladder
OT: Genesis 28:12,17 the ladder between earth and heaven.
NT: Colossians 1:20; John 1:51 The cross connecting us to heaven
Joseph
OT: Genesis 37:3 deeply loved by his father
NT: Matthew 3:17 (KJV) Jesus, *...my beloved Son...*

Jesus in the Old Testament

OT: Genesis 37:4 ...*they hated him*...
NT: John 7:7 *The world... hates me*
OT: Genesis 37:5 a prophetic gift
NT: Matthew 24 a prophetic gift
OT: Genesis 37:10 every knee will bow
NT: Philippians 2:10 ...*every knee will bow*
OT: Genesis 37:18 brothers plotted to kill him
NT: Matthew 12:14 brothers plotted to kill him
OT: Genesis 37:11,19,20 jealousy caused betrayal
NT: Matthew 27:18 betrayed because of envy
OT: Genesis 37:23,24 held in cistern
NT: Psalm 88 prophetic of Caiaphas' cistern?
OT: Genesis 37:28 sold for silver as a slave
NT: Matthew 26:15 sold for the price of a slave
OT: Genesis 37:28 traders took him down into Egypt
NT: Matthew 2:13 take the young child to Egypt
OT: Genesis 39:17,18 falsely accused
NT: Matthew 26:60 falsely accused
  Joseph was also judged with two men, one of which went to a place to serve the king. The other was condemned. Consider the comparison to the thieves on the crosses.
OT: Genesis 41:46 Joseph was 30 when he began his ministry.
NT: Luke 3:23 Jesus was 30 when he began His ministry.
OT: Genesis 41:57 The world comes to Joseph for bread to live.
NT: John 6:35 The world must come to Jesus, the bread of life, if they would live.
OT: Genesis 42:8 Joseph was unrecognized by his brothers.
NT: 1Corinthians 2:8 unrecognized by the princes of this world
OT: Genesis 45:4 reveals himself to brothers

NT: Revelation 1:7 *Parousia* – His appearing or revealing to the world
OT: Genesis 45:5,7 Sent ahead to save
NT: Hebrews 2:10 "Captain" in Greek is the same as trailblazer, the one who goes ahead.
OT: Genesis 45:8 Joseph is made lord and ruler.
NT: Acts 2:36 Jesus is Lord and Christ and rules in us.
OT: Genesis 45:20 made a place for them
NT: John 14:1,2; Matthew 6:19 Get it?!
OT: Genesis 50:20 What appeared to be evil was ultimately for good.
NT: Colossians 2:15 Jesus triumphed over evil via the cross.

Pharez
Genesis 38:27-29

While the last type, Joseph, was so fully and easily seen. This Pharez shadow or type is almost more of a prophecy. The rabbis see great significance in what was said about Pharez or Perez. "The Midrash highlights Perez, whom we find in the genealogy in Matthew 1:3 and the account in Genesis 38. The phrase "another seed from another place" is used again, in reference to Perez." Remember the seed of the woman in Genesis 3?

"The Midrach Rabbah describes as follows the new phase which began with Perez: 'This is the history of Perez, and it has a profound significance. …When the Holy One created his world there was as yet no Angel of Death… But when Adam and Eve fell into sin, all generations were corrupted. When Perez arose, history began to be fulfilled through him, because from him the Messiah would arise, and in his days the Holy One would cause death to be swallowed up as it is written, 'He will destroy death forever' (Isaiah 5:28)."

Ben Parets refers to the Messiah as 'son of Perez'. Since Judah begat Perez or Phares, Jesus is, in a sense, the 'Son of Perez'. Midrash Tanhuma states, "Thus Judah profited, because from him came forth Perez and Hezron from whom are descended David and the Messiah King, he who will save Israel."

Rabbi Moses Ben Nahman who lived towards the end of the 13th century, describes the birth of Perez as follows: "He was encircled by a hedge, and he was enclosed within it. That is why it is said 'So this is how you have broken through the hedge and come out from within it'. Perez was the first-born, 'The first-born through the power of the Most High, as it is written, 'I will give to him a first-born son'. This was written about the holy person who is to come, David, the King of Israel–long may he live. Those who are wise will understand."

Breaking out of the hedge depicts when Christianity broke out of the Judaic legalism. The rabbis speak a great deal about the hedge of the Law. There are 613 commands and prohibitions in the Old Testament. See Micah 2:12-13 and Ephesians 2:14-15.

Rabbi Shlomo Yitshak (1040-1105) said of Perez that he is "their savior, the one who will break open the way". Rabbi David Qimhi declares that "the one who breaks open the way is Elijah, and their king is the Branch, the Son of David" (Messianic terms).

The writings of some of the most widely recognized Jewish exegetes in reference to Perez help us to see clearly that the Messiah was One who would break the hedge of the Law. It is not by keeping the Law we are saved but faith in the One who fulfilled it for us, making a way for us, our Trailblazer – King Jesus, descendent of Perez. (Hebrews 2:10)

Jesus in Exodus
Part 1

Since you have seen the three main ways we see Jesus in Genesis, we will proceed to Exodus and cover the revelations in order without separating them by category. Now that we have these fundamentals in place, we'll move along at a faster pace. Exodus is known as the Book of Redemption. The spiritual significance is quite obvious with Israel as the people of God, Moses the Deliverer, and Egypt representing the world. With this analogy in mind we see that the only One who can deliver us from bondage to sin is, of course, Jesus the Christ. He delivers us from bondage to this present evil world. (Galatians 1:4)

Moses, the prominent figure of Exodus, is clearly a shadow of Jesus. In rabbinical writings, one of the most common parallels is that of Moses and the Messiah. The reason for this is the prophetic word of Moses in Deuteronomy 18:15,18,19. *[15] The LORD your God will raise up for you a prophet like me from among your own brothers. You must listen to him. [18] I will raise up for them a prophet like you from among their brothers; I will put my words in his mouth, and he will tell them everything I command him. [19] If anyone does not listen to my words that the prophet speaks in my name, I myself will call him to account.*
Some rabbis believe this refers to Joshua, but many see it predicting the Messiah. The prophecy indicates that He will speak in the name of God and with His authority. An interesting quote from the Targums in reference to this prophecy alludes to the virgin birth. "A prophet I will raise up from amongst your brethren <u>through</u> the Holy Spirit." (emphasis mine)

The similarities begin with his birth amidst the slaying of many infants, he alone being spared. It continues with him fleeing the death threat of the ruling power. When Moses arrived in Midian, he drove off shepherds that were keeping the people from the water. That reminds us of Jesus' interaction with the Pharisees. He heard God's voice at the Burning Bush and began his role as the deliverer and leader of his people. With Jesus it was at the baptism by John and also hearing the voice of God. "Thou art my beloved Son …" Moses returned to Egypt on a donkey to deliver the people. Jesus entered Jerusalem on a donkey to deliver mankind.

Moses was familiar with two worlds, Egypt and Israelite culture. Jesus is familiar with earth and heaven. Moses led the people to a place that looked like death. Jesus leads us to death to ourselves. The people were, in a sense, baptized in the Red Sea. (1Corinthians 10:1,2) He led them to bitter water but made it sweet.

Is that not true of Jesus in your life, leading you through difficult experiences that are made sweet with His presence? He gave them the words of God from the mountain. That reminds us of the Sermon on the Mount. He interceded over and over for the people. Jesus ever lives to make intercession for us. He brought them to the Promised Land. Jesus guides us to a Promised Land here in this life in the Spirit and to our eternal Promised Land in heaven. (Hebrews 12:22) He married a Cushite which caused a family dispute. (Numbers 12:1) The bride of Christ includes Gentiles, which

caused a dispute with the early Jewish Christians. Moses was the most humble man on the face of the earth. (Numbers 12:3 compare to Philippians 2:5-8) They each made

Jesus in the Old Testament

themselves of no reputation to serve the Father. I'm sure I'm missing many other comparisons. Why not take the time to look for a few of your own?

The Burning Bush
This is a theophany that is not a bodily form.

¹ Now Moses was tending the flock of Jethro his father-in-law, the priest of Midian, and he led the flock to the far side of the desert and came to Horeb, the mountain of God. ² There the angel of the LORD appeared to him in flames of fire from within a bush. Moses saw that though the bush was on fire it did not burn up. ³ So Moses thought, "I will go over and see this strange sight--why the bush does not burn up." ⁴ When the LORD saw that he had gone over to look, God called to him from within the bush, "Moses! Moses!" And Moses said, "Here I am." ⁵ "Do not come any closer," God said. "Take off your sandals, for the place where you are standing is holy ground." ⁶ Then he said, "I am the God of your father, the God of Abraham, the God of Isaac and the God of Jacob." At this, Moses hid his face, because he was afraid to look at God. ⁷ The LORD said, "I have indeed seen the misery of my people in Egypt. I have heard them crying out because of their slave drivers, and I am concerned about their suffering. (Exodus 3:1-7)

Notice the reference to the Angel of the LORD in verse two. Here we see a visible manifestation of God that communicated the will and calling of God to Moses. It's a common little thorn bush ablaze with the glory of God. What a picture of the incarnation! (1John 1:1) The heart of the Father is for you to become a little burning bush. Get on fire for Jesus and the world will come to watch you burn. In the process, they will encounter the Living God. In Exodus 3:14, when Moses asks His name, He said, "*I am that I am...*". You see this name again in the seven (the number implies perfect, complete) *"I am"* of the book of John. They include the Bread of Life, Light of the World, the Door, the Good Shepherd, the Resurrection and the Life, the Way the Truth and the Life, and the True Vine.

When the woman at the well asked about the Messiah Jesus response was "I am He." In the Greek it is simply – "I AM!" Speaking to the religious leaders He said, *"Before Abraham was, I AM"* (John 8:58 KJV). The verse that follows says they took up stones to stone Him. They knew perfectly well the claim He was making. When the soldiers came to arrest him and asked for Jesus of Nazareth, He responded the same way, *"I AM".* John 18:6 The force of that is what knocked them to the ground. We'll save the items of Passover for the next chapter and go on to the next types.

The Bread from Heaven
Exodus 16:4 KJV *Behold I will rain bread from heaven for you.* Jesus clearly taught that He was the true bread from heaven. (John 6:48-51) He was declaring Himself to be the reality of which the manna was merely a picture. Just as Israel had to daily gather the manna for themselves, so we too must daily feed upon Jesus. Have you developed a habit of feeding your soul daily? Does your time go beyond study to actually letting the Word speak to you? That has been the habit of fruitful men and women of God.

The Rock
Compare Exodus 17:6 with 1Corinthians 10:4. The LORD is called our ROCK in Scripture. God gave the command for Him to be stricken. See Isaiah 53:4. He was a river of life poured out. Just as the water from the rock gave life to the

people, so the water, Jesus, gives spiritual life to those dying in sin.

The second time there was a need for water, Moses was told to speak to the rock. (Numbers 20:8-11) Instead, he smote the Rock twice. What a powerful analogy! Since Jesus has been stricken by God for our sins, we now need to but ask for His living water. Moses ruined the picture by disobedience, and because of that, He was not allowed to enter the Promised Land. When you get spiritually thirsty, you only need to go to Him and ask, and you will be filled. (Matthew 5:6)

That water that came from the Rock is also a type of Christ. Jesus does not give us 'things' that meet our need, He gives us Himself. (John 7:37-38)

The Law
The Law is a shadow of the good things to come (Hebrews 10:1) and all good things are summed up in the Son. Just as the Law was given by Moses, grace and truth came by Jesus Christ. (John 1:17) The Law told us what was required by God and Jesus met that requirement. Just as Moses gave us the laws, Jesus gave us a new command. The hundreds of rules became one great command, "love".

We will go on to look at Jesus in the Passover in the next chapter and after that, Jesus in the Tabernacle. Are you daily gathering the Bread which came down from heaven? Are you standing on the unshakable Rock and asking Him for your daily supply of life giving water? Is the new command on your heart and mind and lips, just as the Law was suppose to be to the Israelites?

Jesus in Exodus
Part 2
The Feasts of Israel

The books of Exodus and Leviticus tell of a number of feasts and holidays the Jews were to observe each year. Since these feasts are dictated to Moses from God and called the LORD's, surely these feasts and holidays look forward to something about the Son of God as well. The Apostle Paul said as much in his letter to Colossians. *[16] Therefore do not let anyone judge you by what you eat or drink, or with regard to a religious festival, a New Moon celebration or a Sabbath day. [17] These are a shadow of the things that were to come; the reality, however, is found in Christ.* (Colossians 2:16-17) We'll take a look at each shadow and see the reality in Jesus.

Passover and Unleavened Bread
Leviticus 23:4-8 and Exodus 12:1-4, 15-20
Every time Christians celebrate communion, they are seeing Passover as fulfilled in Jesus and the Last Supper. This was one of three feasts that required mandatory attendance. Is that because it is so filled with pictures of Jesus?

Just as Moses was the deliverer of God's people in Egypt, so Jesus delivers us from bondage to sin. We recognize His body and blood as the Lamb of God that takes away the sins of the world and brings us out from under the wrath of God. Just as the blood on the doorposts protected the Children of Israel, so now the blood of Jesus is the atonement that rescues us from the just wrath of God. And just as the

Children of Israel were commanded to eat all of the lamb, so Jesus insisted that we must eat His flesh and drink His blood to have eternal life. (John 6:54) He was not speaking of cannibalism, or of the comm.-union elements literally becoming His flesh and blood, but as the Word made flesh (John 1:14), He was speaking of receiving the Word of God.

As Jesus led the disciples in the Passover meal that we know as the Last Supper, He applied two of the elements to Himself. He declared the unleavened bread to represent His sinless body, and the cup of redemption to be His blood.

The word that is translated Passover is *pasach.* In (Isaiah 31:5 KJV) the word is used in reference to a bird. *He will pass over and preserve it.* The picture of the Hebrew word for Passover is like a bird fluttering over her brood to protect them. Jehovah stood guard over the doors with the blood of the Lamb as the angel of death passed by. Jesus wanted to do this for Jerusalem, but they would not come to Him. (Matthew 23:37)

<u>The Passover Lamb</u>
Exodus 12:5-7,46
The Passover lamb had to be killed for its blood to be effective in keeping them from death. It was the blood of the Savior who died for us that keeps us from death. It was to be an unblemished lamb, so the people watched it for four days to be sure it was perfect. Jesus entered Jerusalem for the last time on the very day lambs were to be selected. He was offering Himself as the Lamb of God.

Only a perfect lamb could make atonement. In the same way, Jesus' public ministry presented a man whose earthly judge, Pilate, said, *I find no fault in Him,* John 18:38 (KJV).

Hebrews 4:15 tells us He passed all the tests man faces without sin. (1Peter 1:18,19) No bones of the lamb were to be broken. (John 19:36; Psalm 34:20) Jesus was pierced instead of having His legs broken as was customary to hasten death of the crucified. (Exodus 12:3) There are more than thirty New Testament references to Jesus as the Lamb of God.

Bitter Herbs
Exodus 12:8
Bitterness reminded them of the bitter hardships of slavery in Egypt, but it also looked forward to an even more bitter time to come. (Zechariah 12:10) When Israel has the veil lifted and understands they rejected and killed their Messiah, they will grieve bitterly. (Zechariah 13:9) Then they will call on His name and say, "The Lord is our God".

Unleavened Bread
The Unleavened Bread was a picture of Jesus. During the week of Unleavened Bread (Hag HaMatzot), the people ate only bread without leaven. Jesus told the Jews that He was the living bread that people would eat and not die. (John 6:48-50)

The lack of leaven symbolized their haste in departure, not having time to allow the bread to rise, but there is a deeper meaning. Leaven in Scripture almost always refers to sin. For the next week, they were not to eat bread that had yeast. When we come to Christ as our Redeemer, we are to put sin out of our lives. The old nature must die with Jesus on the Cross. We are to be sanctified and no longer walk according to our sinful desires. Leaven in Hebrew means 'bitter' or 'sour'. Sin has that same affect in our lives. When we allow it to continue, it makes us bitter or sour. It also puffs up making it bigger but not changing the weight. The parallel is thinking more of ourselves than we ought. (Romans 12:3)

The ancient Hebrews made leavened bread using the same method that we use today to make sourdough bread. Once the yeast had worked through the dough, a piece was set aside for the next batch. Batch after batch each new generation of yeast in the bread had descended from the original yeast spores. Sin has leavened the human race. It has been passed down from Adam to us. (1Corinthians 5:6-8)

The word for 'unleavened' is *matzo* which means 'sweet, without sourness'. It pictures the sinless life of our Savior who fulfilled all righteousness. His sweet life was an example for us of walking in the Spirit. When the Temple was destroyed, the rabbis declared the *matzo* to be a memorial of the Passover Lamb. Without realizing it, the Jews have followed Jesus change in the celebration of Passover. ...*Do this in remembrance of me.* (Luke 22:19) We take the bread of communion to remember the bodily sacrifice of our Lord. He was the pure, sweet, sinless Lamb, the Lamb of God. Have you selected Him? No other sacrifice will satisfy the justice of God.

Firstfruits
On the second day of Unleavened Bread, the people celebrated Firstfruits. (Leviticus 23:9-14) On Passover, observant Jews would mark the grain standing in the field that was to be dedicated to the Lord. On the first day of Unleavened Bread, they harvested and prepared that sheaf. Then on the third day, the second day of Unleavened Bread, called Yom HaBikkurim, they brought that first ripe sheaf of barley to the Temple. This offering showed that they trusted

God to bring the rest of the harvest and that the first and best was God's. The priest would then wave it before the Lord.

This was the very day that Jesus was raised from the dead. We celebrate Yom HaBikkurim every year as Resurrection Day, also known as Easter. The Apostle Paul saw this connection and called Jesus the firstfruits from among the dead. (1Corinthians 15:20-23) That makes believers in Jesus the rest of the harvest. Passover, Unleavened Bread, and Firstfruits were each the shadow of the reality we find in Jesus. They painted a picture not only of His first coming but also of when He will come again and take us to be with Him.

<u>The Blood on the Door</u>
Take a bunch of hyssop, dip it into the blood in the basin and put some of the blood on the top and on both sides of the doorframe. Not one of you shall go out the door of his house until morning."
(Exodus 12:22)

The basin mentioned is not like we would think of the word today. It is the Egyptian word *sap*. It was a ditch in front of the door threshold to keep rainwater out of the house. A container was placed in it to prevent seepage. The Passover Lamb was slain there in front of the door. Hyssop was placed in this 'basin' at the base of the door and then the header was marked and then each side of the door. The sign of the cross was made in doing so. The crown of thorns drew blood from Jesus' head that also sweat drops of blood. The nails pierced the hands and feet. *I am the door, whoever enters in through me will be saved...* (John 10:9a KJV) And so, centuries before Jesus, people entered by the blood stained door as death passed them by. In the morning they stepped out into a new life on their way to a new place, delivered.

Passover Conditions
All the congregation of Israel must eat the Passover. (Exodus 12:47) No one who was a stranger, or uncircumcised, or outside the covenant, could participate. See Exodus 12:43-45. (Communion is only open to those who have entered into the new covenant, Jeremiah 31:31-33.) There was to be a lamb for each household. It could include the extended family as long as they are living under one roof. See Exodus 12:46. (We see family conversions in the book of Acts – also consider Rahab and family) Jesus is salvation for our whole family.

They must eat the Passover entirely. Nothing could be left by morning. (Exodus 34:25) There is no partial salvation, no "kind of" believing. They had to put away leaven from their tables and houses for seven days. (Exodus 13:6,7) We have discussed the picture of sanctification. All the first-born who had been redeemed by the blood of the lamb were sanctified to the Lord. (1Corinthians 6:19,20)

The calendar of the Jews began with the first Passover, and so it is with us. Our life begins when we come under Christ. We are a new creation from the time the blood is put on the doorpost of our hearts. (2Corinthians 5:17; Romans 6:8-14)

Seder Traditions
The rabbis regarded the words of the ancient sages almost as highly as the Torah. These oral traditions were compiled in a book in the 1st or 2nd century A.D. called the Mishnah. One of the things it covers is the order of the celebration of Passover. Seder means order of service. One of the additions

to the original Passover was four cups of wine. Heated water was added to them. What a picture of the blood that was shed for us that flowed from His side. (John 19:34)

It was also a symbol of joy. It was believed that just as God delivered them from Egypt at Passover, and the Law given in the same season, so the Messiah would come at Passover. We see almost all of the elements of the 1st century Seder at the Last Supper. It is interesting to note that Judas left before eating the Paschal lamb. The tradition of the time was to eat nothing after the lamb, but only to drink the last two cups of wine. Jesus however added a shocking new element when after the supper he took the bread and broke it and said, *...This is my body, which is broken for you...* (1Corinthians 11:24 KJV). After the temple was destroyed, the Jews would add this tradition, but Jesus was the first to use what became known as the *aphikomen* or after-dish.

Then he took the cup. This was the third of the four cups of wine. Only the first and the third are mentioned in the gospels. The third was the most significant according to the Mishnah. It symbolized the blood of the Lamb and was called the Cup of Redemption. It was of this cup that Jesus said, *...This is the cup of the new covenant in my blood which is shed for you.* (Luke 22:20)

The four cups of the Passover represent the four "I will" in Exodus 6:6b-7a. *[6b] ...I will bring you out from under the yoke of the Egyptians. I will free you from being slaves to them, and I will redeem you with an outstretched arm and with mighty acts of judgment. [7a] I will take you as my own people, and I will be your God...* Now do you see why Jesus said He would not drink the fourth cup until He drank it anew with us in His Father's kingdom? The fourth cup is the

Marriage Feast of the Lamb when takes us to be His own people and forever becomes our God. It is the cup of consummation.

In the contemporary Seder there are even more pictures, as God is still trying to reveal his Son to the Children of Israel. The unleavened bread or matzo is put in a special bag with three compartments for three pieces. If a family does not own one of these bags, they may be placed one on the other on a tray. They symbolize unity, but various reasons are given as to what unity. There is a small cup that will be filled four times with sweet wine. Early rabbis say this represents the four verbs in Exodus 6:6,7. There is a shank bone of a lamb to remind them of the Passover Lamb. Two larger silver goblets are placed at the table. One is for the host and the other at an empty chair. The chair is for Elijah, who will announce the coming of the Messiah. (Malachi 4:5) The host dons a white cotton or silk robe that is reminiscent of the priestly garment, but also of the robe of righteousness that is ours through our Passover Lamb. The host serves the bitter herbs, to be dipped in salt water reminding us of tears. Then he takes the middle matzo out and breaks it in half. He replaces half, and while the children cover their eyes, he wraps the other half in a napkin and hides (or buries) it. This hidden half of the middle wafer is the *aphikomen*.

There are some Psalms recited, and the ritual continues. Then dinner is served. After the feast it is time to hunt for the *aphikomen*. The adults give hints as the children hunt. Once it is found it is given to the host and the Seder continues. It is broken into olive size portions and is the last thing eaten. The third and fourth cup of wine follow along with Psalm 126. It is filled with Messianic predictions. There are prayers for the return of Elijah and even a peek out the door to see if those prayers are answered that night. When the door is opened everyone recites, *Blessed is He who comes in the name of the Lord...* (Psalm 118:26). In Jesus' day, the ceremony ended with the singing of the last Hillel Psalm, 118.

I have left out many of the details, some of which refer to the coming Messiah. But presently we are looking for the shadows and types. Do the children ask why there are three wafers? Does anyone guess as to why the second one is broken? And why is it hidden only to be brought back at the end of the feast?

We know. Someday they will know too. The three are the Trinity who are three in one. Jesus is the Lamb of God who was broken for our redemption. He was buried, hidden from our sight, but was discovered alive after three days. He ascended into heaven, hidden from our view. John the Baptist came in the spirit and power of Elijah to announce the first coming of the Lord. Will that same spirit return as one of the sackcloth prophets to announce the Second Coming in power and glory?

The Passover and Exodus also foreshadow our deliverance from the world at the rapture of the church. Whether this happens before the tribulation or in the midst or end of it, the trumpet will sound and we will be transformed as we meet the Lord in the air. We will again escape the wrath of God upon the earth, just as those within the bloodstained doors escaped God's wrath upon Egypt and just as we escaped wrath upon our sins when we fled to our Deliverer on the cross.

Feast of Weeks/Pentecost
Leviticus 23:15-22

The Feast of Weeks or Shavuot was held fifty days after Passover. Each Sabbath the congregation was reminded of the count. After seven full weeks were completed, the fiftieth day (Pentecost in Greek) was celebrated. It was one of the three feasts in which all Jewish males were to come to Jerusalem to celebrate. (Deuteronomy 16:16) The first summer wheat was ripening and the worshiper would bring two loaves made of that first ripe grain and yeast. It was an offering of gratitude to God for the harvest. The priest would wave the loaves along with two lambs for a fellowship offering.

The feast also celebrates Matin Torah. It is believed that this is the time of year in which Moses received the Ten Commandments. Today it is seen as God's marriage covenant with Israel, the Torah being the wedding contract (ketubah). Some syngagues celebrate the day like an actual wedding and for the contract read the following passages: *[19] And I will betroth thee unto me for ever; yea, I will betroth thee unto me in righteousness, and in judgment, and in lovingkindness, and in mercies. [20] I will even betroth thee unto me in faithfulness: and thou shalt know the LORD*. Hosea 2:19-20 (KJV) *[31] Behold, the days come, saith the LORD, that I will make a new covenant with the house of Israel, and with the house of Judah:* Jeremiah 31:31 (KJV)

The fascinating connection with Jesus is that Jesus is bridegroom and the church is the bride. He is the one that declared the New Covenant was made in His blood. The Spirit that descended on the day of this Feast was the seal of our relationship with Jesus as His bride.

On the Feast of Weeks after the Passover when Jesus was crucified, the disciples were gathered in the upper room. The Holy Spirit was poured out upon them and they heard the sound of a mighty rushing wind and saw flames of fire that settled over each of them. It was the outpouring of the Spirit predicted by Joel the prophet in Joel 2:28-32. Peter stepped outside the upper room and preached to the crowd that had been drawn by the sound. After the message that was understood in every language represented, 3000 people believed and were baptized. (Acts 2:41) This was the firstfruits of the church. These 3000 along with about 500 disciples of Jesus were the beginning of the church. (James 1:18)

It is also significant that there is a fellowship offering on this feast. As Moses received the Law while in fellowship with God, so the Holy Spirit now helps us to understand the Word and keeps us in fellowship with the Father. (John 14:26)

The Feast of Trumpets
Leviticus 23:23-25; Numbers 21:9-6
Rosh Hashanah is the Jewish civil New Year. It is followed by ten days of repentance. Those ten days are followed by the Day of Atonement. Jewish tradition describes these ten days as crucial to whether or not each person's name is written in the Book of Life for another year. It is believed that God looks into your thoughts and actions over the past year during those ten days. If your good deeds outweigh the bad, then on the Day of Atonement your name goes in the Book of Life for another year, which is why it is also called the Day of Judgment. This is relating to earthly judgment not eternal judgment.

Jewish believers in the tradition spend much of those ten days repenting in a synagogue to earn a little extra favor before the final decision day. The services of those ten days include about 100 soundings of the shofar, and thus the name Feast of Trumpets. The sounding of the trumpets is a call to remembrance. Scripture does not say to whom or exactly what is to be remembered, but tradition has interpreted it as reminding the people to offer their lives to God, to have faith in the future coming Messiah, and faith in their return to the land of their fathers.

Very little of this comes directly from Scripture. Instead, it is based on tradition from rabbinical writings. Since this feast has become one centered around the concern of judgment, we should see just who it is that is the Judge. The Father has entrusted all judgment to the Son. This is Jesus' own declaration. One day we will all stand before Jesus, and He won't be weighing our good deeds against our bad ones. Here is Jesus' explanation as to how that judgment is based.
[22] Moreover, the Father judges no one, but has entrusted all judgment to the Son, [23] that all may honor the Son just as they honor the Father. He who does not honor the Son does not honor the Father, who sent him. [24] "I tell you the truth, whoever hears my word and believes him who sent me has eternal life and will not be condemned; he has crossed over from death to life."
(John 5:22-24)

Judgment is based on what we do with Jesus, not our deeds, for by the works of the Law no one will be justified. We've all sinned and fallen short of the perfection God requires. If we honor what Jesus has done for us by taking the judgment for our sins, we honor the Father. We pass from death to life and will not be condemned. That is the

Father's gift to us. To reject it is to dishonor God. Those ten days of awe should be spent in worship and wonder that God could atone for our sins with such a merciful gift. (Similar to the Christian period of Lent) It reminds the Jews to offer their lives to God. It reminds us that we have given ourselves as living sacrifices in response to what Jesus did for us. (Romans 12:1-2) It reminds them the Messiah is coming. It reminds us that He came and experienced everything that we do so that He could be a merciful and just High Priest. It reminds the Jews of their return to the Promised Land. It reminds us that our Promised Land of heaven, in God's presence for all eternity, is nearer than when we first believed. (Romans 13:11)

Unlike Abraham who was spared the sacrifice of his own son, God so loved the world that He gave His one and only Son that we might have the righteousness of God in Him. Our names are in the Lamb's book of life (Revelation 21:27) not only for a year but for all eternity, and for that, we will praise His name forever! (John 10:28-29)

Finally it reminds us of the last great trumpet blast.

The Day of Atonement
Leviticus 23:26-32
The book of Leviticus revolves around the Great Day of Atonement or Yom Kippur in chapter 16. It came only once a year. It was a time when the community awareness of sin was heightened, and humility was the attitude of the day. It took two goats to represent death and resurrection on this special Day. One was slain on the altar, and the other had the sins of the people placed upon it and was driven into the wilderness, separated from them.

Of course, this ritual only looked forward to the real Day of Atonement on Calvary. (Hebrews 10:4; 2Corinthians 5:19) The flesh of the sin offering was burned outside the camp. (Hebrews 13:12,13) The same cross that gained us access to God has taken us out of the camp of the world, separated unto God.

Jewish tradition holds that there was a scarlet yarn around the head of the scapegoat. You can't help but wonder if those observing the crucifixion did not see the similarity with the crown of thorns.

The scarlet yarn was hung in the Temple and mysteriously turned white during the year showing that God had accepted the sacrifice. Jewish records tell us that for some reason this miraculous event stopped in 30 A.D. They were still looking to the shadow and not the reality that had come.

The Feast of Booths
Leviticus 23:33:42
The Feast of Booths or Tabernacles, also known as Sukkot, included three principle experiences; refreshment, rejoicing and rest. In all three themes we have a clear intersection with the message of Jesus in the Gospel of John. The following is from an article in *Israel My Glory* by Steve Colon volume 59 number 5 Sept/Oct 2001.

    A second fascinating ceremony associated with the Feast of Tabernacles involved lights. Each afternoon of the seven days, priests and pilgrims gathered at the Court of the Women. Four large oil lamps illuminated the court. It was said that the light from these lamps was so bright it penetrated every courtyard in Jerusalem.

As the women watched from the upper terraces, the "men of piety and good works used to dance before the oil lamps with burning torches in their hands, singing songs and praises." Meanwhile, "countless levites played on harps, lyres, cymbals and trumpets and instruments of music" (Mishnah Sukkot 5:4). The light festivities continued all night until dawn.

The illumination from these imposing Temple lamps symbolized two realities. The first was the reality of the "Light of all Lights"- the Shekinah Glory – the visible presence of God that filled the first Temple, which Solomon built (1 Kiings 8:10-11). The second was Ha'or Gadol (the Great Light) who would soon come and bring light to those who were spiritually dead and dwelling in darkness (Isaiah 9:2).

Jesus was at the Temple. Perhaps it was during the light celebration or when the lights were extinguished on the eighth day that He said for all to hear, "I am the light of the world; he that followeth me shall not walk in darkness, but shall have the light of life" (John 8:12). He proclaimed two truths with this statement: (1) He is the "Great Light" who the prophet Isaiah said would come, and (2) He is God in the flesh and the Glory of the Temple (cf. John 1:14).

The response was threefold. Some religious people rejected Him (John 8:13), others were inquisitive enough to ask Him for more information (John 8:25), and still others believed and received him (John 8:30). The joy associated with the lights and water ritual of the Feast of Tabernacles anticipated Jesus' coming and bringing light to a dark, sinful world.

(Editor: Here is a brief explanation of the water ceremony. A priest would take a golden pitcher out of the south gate or Water Gate of the Temple and go to the pool of Siloam in musical procession. He filled it as he quoted Isaiah 12:3. When people asked about the significance of the ceremony, they were told that it was symbolic of the pouring out of the Holy Spirit. Returning to the Temple, the priest would join with another priest who had a pitcher of wine. They poured them out on the altar through silver funnels while women sang the Hallel Psalms 113-118. The priests marched around the altar with willow branches reciting Psalm 118:25. Then everyone fell silent to consider the symbolism and sense their personal need of refreshment from God. This went on for seven days, but on the seventh day there was a greater intensity, called the Great Praise Day. This time the priests would go around the altar seven times before the drink offering was poured out. It was probably at this time that Jesus shouted (John 7:37-38). WOW! Imagine how irritated the priests must have been. pdw) The article from *Israel My Glory* by Peter Colon continues below.

In ancient times, the eighth day of the Feast of Tabernacles was called the "Last Good Day." Viewed as a Sabbath, it was designed as a time to rest and reflect on the spiritual significance of the seven-day jubilation. Special activities took place at the Temple. The priests offered the daily and special Sabbath sacrifices (Numbers 28:9-10), while others recited Psalm 92, the Sabbath song anticipating the blessings of the Messianic Kingdom. Lingering in the minds and hearts of everyone during the entire weeklong celebration was, no doubt, the expectation that, at any moment, God could establish the great Sukkah Shalom (Tabernacle of Peace).

"For thou, LORD, hast made me glad through thy work: I will triumph in the works of thy hands" (Psalms 92:4). When the festivities had all ceased, Jesus again came to the Temple – this time to perform an awesome work with His hands. He gave sight to a man born blind (John 9). Everyone knew this kind of miracle required divine intervention. After anointing the man's eyes with clay from the ground, Jesus instructed him, "Go wash in the pool of Siloam (which by interpretation is Sent). He [the blind man] went his way, therefore, and washed, and came back seeing" (v.7).

Jesus sent the blind man to the same pool the priest with the golden pitcher had fetched water from each day of the Feast. Jesus was teaching that it is the Holy Spirit, represented by water and whom He alone can give, who opens the eyes of all who are spiritually blind. The text also states, "And it was the Sabbath day when Jesus made the clay, and opened his eyes" (v.14).

Jesus performed this miracle to validate everything He had said and done during the Feast of Tabernacles. By doing the impossible, He proved His words could be trusted and that He was God in the flesh, the Messiah of Israel, the true dispenser of the Holy Spirit, and the only source of light and life. Mankind no longer has to fumble blindly in this world. True rest for the wanderer is available in Jesus Christ.

Rejoicing in the Law
Leviticus 23:36

Simchat Torah literally means rejoicing over the Law. When the annual reading of the first five books of the Bible is completed on the 23rd of Tishri (22nd in Israel) there is a great celebration in synagogues. This holiday was not observed until the 9th or 10th century. It is not mandated in the Torah but is still a longstanding Jewish tradition. The celebration of God's word is something to which we can surely relate.

The Torah is divided into 54 sections so that it can be read through completely in each year. Simchat Torah is the celebration that takes place before that last reading. There is dancing, clapping and singing as the Torah scrolls are paraded around the synagogue seven times. The men are all called to the front to take their turn reading from the scrolls. The most honored person of the evening is the one who reads the final portion of the first scroll – the end of that year's Torah readings. He is called the bridegroom of the Torah. It is his responsibility to provide a feast for the congregation after the beginning of the next year's readings and the reading from the prophets is completed.

Though this is not mandated in Scripture, we can see Jesus in several ways. He is the Word made flesh. (John 1:14) Certainly we are to "rejoice in the Lord always…" Many Christian congregations also read the Bible in one year, both the Old and New Testaments. The feast provided by the final reader reminds us that the Bridegroom, Christ Jesus, will provide for us the Marriage Supper of the Lamb. What a day of rejoicing that will be!

<u>Feast of Dedication</u>
John 10:22
We are more familiar with this feast by its Jewish name, Hanukkah. It runs from the 25th of Kislev to the 2nd of Tevet. This feast is not in the Torah but was celebrated by Jesus in John 10:22. In the 2nd century before Jesus, the Seleucids, led by Antiochus Epiphanes (god manifest) had conquered Israel and defiled the Temple. There were strict penalties imposed on anyone who did not give up Jewish ways and practice Greek customs. The Maccabees led a revolt and defeated the Syrians to take back the nation in 165 BC. As they cleansed and rededicated the Temple, they found only enough oil to light the sacred lampstand for one day. However, God made the oil sufficient to burn for eight days, the time required for the dedication of new oil.

The feast is a time to remember that God delivered them from their enemies and graciously provided for them when they were earnest in re-establishing the Temple worship. It also reminds the faithful not to compromise with the world regardless of the cost.

How can this feast foreshadow Jesus? Oddly enough it was at this feast that Jesus declared that He and the Father are one. (John 10:30) In other words, He is God in the flesh. That was the claim of the Syrian that caused all the trouble, Antiochus Epiphanes. The great difference of course is that Antiochus is dead, but Jesus is alive! The counterfeit came before the real thing.

The focus of the feast is the miracle of God providing light to the lampstand. Jesus told us clearly that He is the Light of the world. He is the eternal flame of the Minorah. He is the miraculous provision of God.

The second key focus of the feast is the refusal to compromise with the world. Though they did not understand it at the time, the world had crept into Jewish legalism. The many laws to protect the laws were man's way of worshipping his own ability to keep himself "pure". Jesus is the only One that lived a life without compromise with this world. He never gave in to the temptations of sensuality or of religious pride. His example is the only pure example of true separation to God alone. He is the miraculous provision of light. He is the uncompromising One.

Jesus in Exodus
Part 3
The Tabernacle

If you think these many types and shadows of Jesus is stretching things to see something that was not originally intended, let me remind you that, in many cases, we are seeing a New Testament confirmation that tells us this was indeed by God's design. In the case of the Tabernacle, we have the certainty of Hebrews 8:5. *They (the priests) serve at a sanctuary that is a copy and shadow of what is in heaven.* By now you are probably wondering if I see Jesus in everything – not yet, but someday by God's grace... God's heart is to reveal His Son to us and through us. It is by beholding Him that we are changed into His likeness. (2Corinthians 3:18) Let us look upon Him in the Tabernacle.

The Tabernacle was set up in the center of the Israelite camp. It was a visible manifestation of God's presence. A tent is compared to our body in the New Testament (2Corinthians 5:1). The Tent of Meeting was where the Shekinah of God dwelt with His people. The Shekinah took another body – Jesus of Nazareth, Emmanuel, God with us. John 1:14 literally means, the Word of God became flesh and tabernacled among us, as the Revised Version notes. We would say He camped with us. And again in Revelation 21:3 (KJV), *The tabernacle of God is with men.* Everything in the Temple is to reveal the glory of God to us. (Psalm 29:9)

As we approach the Tabernacle, it looks rather unattractive. The exterior perimeter was of badger skins, which were black. Isaiah 53:2 predicts *…nothing in his appearance that we should desire him.* But the inside was altogether lovely! The entry curtain called "The Gate" and also named "Life" was of scarlet, blue and purple embroidery. It was 20 cubits wide by 5 cubits high to emphasize the entrance is wide for every man that wills to enter in. *Whosoever will let him come…* (Revelation 22:17 KJV)

Inside the outer wall, you are completely surrounded by a curtain of pure white linen, *"complete in Christ Jesus", "made the righteousness of God in Him".* Walking in a straight line from the Gate and you will come to the Altar of Burnt Offering. *One sacrifice for sins for ever.* (Hebrews 10:12 KJV) The altar is most holy. Whatever touches the altar is made holy. (Exodus 29:37; 30:29) Consider Jesus' touch upon the unclean. He was not defiled, but instead made them clean. (Matthew 23:18-19) Jesus is most holy, of which the altar is just a picture.

Straight behind the altar is the Laver for cleansing ritual. See Zechariah 13:1. Every Israelite could come to this point. Have we entered the Gate, accepted the sacrifice, known the cleansing that are each a picture of Jesus and what He is to us?

Only the priests could enter the Tent itself. If we have known the cleansing, we are priests unto God and can enter directly behind the Laver. The curtain that made the entryway into the tent was called "the Door", also known as "Truth". Every blessing must be received by entering through Christ who said He is truth.

Once we have gone through the Gate of Life we should go on through the Door of Truth. Both doors are the Lord Jesus.

Jesus in the Old Testament

In Him are all the riches of heaven. The innermost door is known as "the Veil" or "the Way". All are the same material and the same total yardage. Jesus came from the inside out, from the Holy of Holies out into the world. That is why in describing Himself He uses the order from the inside out, the way, the truth, and the life. He is the entrance to every spiritual thing.

Many stop just inside the Door after coming to the altar. "I have entered the Gate and I am a child of the King. I have heaven, why do I need to go deeper?" Walk into Jesus again, child of the King.

Now, enter the Door. You see the gold plated pillars. They were set in huge silver sockets sunk into the sand. This silver was purchased with the redemption money of Israel. The whole tent rested on the foundation of redemption. (1Peter 1:18,19)

The table of Shewbread or Bread of the Presence is on the right. The Golden Lampstand is on the left. In the Shewbread we see the presence of God, fresh and fragrant. Jesus is the Bread from heaven that God has given for the life of the world. The Golden Lampstand with its seven flames light this inner court. (Revelation 1:4) Jesus is the Light. If we have gone on through the Door, His Presence is with us and His Word is a light to our feet and a lamp to our path. If you aren't experiencing this, go deeper into Jesus. Go into the Holy Place where you have food and light of a spiritual nature.

The priests of the Old Testament could come this far, but they dared not to enter through the Veil. Only the high priest could enter into the Holy of Holies, and that on the Day of

Atonement after he had sacrificed a bull for the sins of himself and his family. (Leviticus 16:32-34) He entered before the Ark of the Covenant with blood and with fear and trepidation. Bells hung around the bottom edge of his sacred robe so that his movements could be heard.

There is no candle here, for the Shekinah rests above the mercy seat flooding the room with light. This was where God met with man. Tradition says a rope was tied around the ankle of the priest so that in the event of the justice of God blowing the life out of him, he could be pulled out of the Holy of Holies without someone else going behind the curtain.

But Christ being come an High Priest of good things to come...by His own blood...has entered into heaven itself, now to appear in the presence of God for us... (Hebrews 9:11-12,24 KJV)

The next chapter tells us that He did this so that we could come boldly to the throne of grace and find help in time of need. (Hebrews 10:19-22)

We have already seen that this last curtain to enter is Christ, but Hebrews 10:20 tells us the curtain is his body. It was torn open on the cross, and what happens to a substance happens to its shadow. And so, the Veil was torn from top to bottom. Imagine the shock of the priests in the Holy Place that day. They must have run for cover. But we don't need to run, for we enter with the precious blood of Christ as our covering. The punishment we so justly deserve fell on Jesus, and so by that justification we can draw near to God without fear of wrath.

In that most holy of places is the golden Altar of Incense. It was listed in the Holy Place in Exodus but is listed in the Holy of Holies in Hebrews. In Revelation 8:3,4 the incense is mentioned with the prayers of the saints. But these avail because of the intercession of Jesus, our Great High Priest. (Hebrews 7:25)

Finally, we are there before the Ark of Covenant. Golden cherubim with wings cover the mercy seat where the Shekinah-glory rests. Hebrews 9:5 calls it an "atonement cover" in the NIV.

Inside are more pictures of Jesus. (Hebrews 9:4) There is the manna, and Jesus is the true bread from heaven. There are the Ten Commandments, and Jesus is the Word made flesh. There is the Rod of Aaron.

The Rod of Aaron was a dead branch made into a staff. (Numbers 17:6-10) When it lay overnight before the Lord, it budded and had almonds to prove that God had chosen the Levites to be priests. What was the proof of who God had chosen to be priest but life from death. The rod was a symbol of authority. The proof that Jesus was the man God chose to be priest forever was His resurrection. All authority in heaven and earth is given to Him. (Matthew 28:18)

This concludes our study of Christ in the book of Exodus. Would you take some time to think about what this means to your life?

Jesus in Leviticus

Genesis showed us how incapable man is. It shows the great need for judgment in the Garden, the flood, and Sodom and Gomorrah. In Exodus we saw the redemption and salvation that was offered to all who would hear. In Moses we saw a type of the Redeemer that would lead us from the captivity of the world.

Leviticus follows with God's estimation of sin. It also contrasts that with the holiness of God and the futility and even danger of trying to approach Him by any other means than atonement.

Over and over this book reminds us of sin and the payment for it through sacrifice. Our culture today is revolted by all the animal sacrifice, but that is because we do not understand the horror of sin. Anything less would lighten the meaning of rebellion against our Creator. As a person truly draws near to God, two things stand out, the utter sinfulness of man and the absolute holiness of God. If sin was not so utterly evil, then the punishment might be something less severe. We see how reprehensible sin is to God when we see how God would have us deal with it, by sacrifice, and how He dealt with it in the ultimate sacrifice of the Cross.

Punishment that fits the crime is justice. The justice of God on sin is the cross.

"Sin is the most expensive thing in the universe, pardoned or unforgiven," C. Finney.

Dr. Guinness said, "To understand the seriousness of sin, we must fathom three oceans, the ocean of human suffering, the ocean of the sufferings of the Lord Jesus Christ, the ocean of future suffering which awaits impenitent sinners."

We cannot get a true sense of the horror that sin really is because we are sinners. Christ alone being sinless, understood it, and the agony of the Garden was His struggle of facing the sheer torment of it. In the history of great revivals, we almost always see intense conviction of sin and sincere repentance.

The main type presented in Leviticus was of animal bloodshed. The reality is Christ on the cross, the Lamb of God.

<u>The Offerings</u>
There are five different types of offerings outlined in Leviticus. In each one there are three things in common: the offering – Christ is the offering (Hebrews 10:10), the priest – Christ is the priest (Hebrews 4:14), and the one who offers the sacrifice – Christ is the one who offers (Titus 2:14).

There are two main offerings, "sweet savor offering" of which the Burnt Offering was chief. It was burned completely as a sweet smelling savor on the Brazen Altar. It was a *whole* burnt offering, which means that nothing was kept back. In it, we see Christ's total submission to His Father. His whole heart, mind and will were given without reservation. (Ephesians 5:2; Psalm 40:8) Jesus, in man's place, was a sweet savor, fulfilling our duty to God.

In the meat offering, flour and oil were added. The flour was the result of bruising or grinding of the wheat kernel. Jesus' life was constantly ground as *He endured such contradiction of sinners against himself.* (Hebrews 12:3 KJV)

The oil, of course, represents the Spirit. Some believe the flour and oil represent our duty to our neighbor. If that is the case, Jesus perfectly fulfilled that also.

The Sin Offering was solely for the atonement of sin. The fat was burned on the altar and the meat burned outside the camp to show that we must put sin away from us. Jesus was the final and perfect sin offering. (Hebrews 9:26; 2Corinthians 5:21; Isaiah 53:10)

The High Priest

Aaron was a type of the Great High Priest to come, Christ Jesus. He was the man of God's choosing. His tribe, the Levites, were also priests to minister to the Lord. We are the reality of that shadow as priests unto God, the brothers of the High Priest, Christ Jesus.

His sons Abihu and Nadab offered strange fire and were consumed. See Numbers 10. The altar fire was lit by the LORD and only its fire was to be used. What a warning to us that we depend on what God has done for us and not try to do things our own way. We cannot substitute our efforts or zeal for the Holy Spirit without dire consequences. (Romans 10:2;
John 6:63)

Laws for Daily Living

It is truly amazing how many of the laws had to do with sanitary conditions. When we read them today, we understand the need for those laws because of the contamination of bacteria. The first doctor to encourage the washing of hands between visits of mothers who too often died giving birth was Dr. Semmelweis. The mortality rate dropped from 15% to less than 2% of the mothers. In 1845 there was no knowledge of germs. We wonder where this doctor with the Jewish name came up with such a strange idea. By the way, he was fired for his strange advise. Leviticus required the washing of hands in "running water" when dealing with those with infectious diseases. If someone had a running sore, they were to wait seven days after the discharge had ceased and then wash clothes and body in running water. (Leviticus 15:13) Until the 20th century, doctors who did wash their hands did so in a bowl, allowing the germs to remain on their hands.

The spiritual parallel would be sin in our life washed away by the fountain of Living Water. (John 4:10-11) Modern science now understands contagious disease, but we have not recognized the contagious nature of sin. A little leaven leavens the whole lump.

<u>The Leper</u>
Leviticus describes dealing with those who had leprosy but are now cured. (Leviticus 14) First an individual had to recognize they were healed from the affliction and then call for the priest. The priest went to examine the leper outside the camp. In the same way Jesus left His home of heaven and came here to meet us in our infected condition. But He came to pronounce us clean, cured, so we could return with Him to His heavenly home. The priest would take two sparrows. Killing one, he would dip the living bird, a scarlet thread, hyssop and cedar wood in its blood. He would sprinkle the cleansed man and let the living bird fly free.

The ceremonial cleansing called for the priest to take two sparrows. Killing one, he would dip the living bird, scarlet thread, hyssop and cedar wood in its blood. He would sprinkle the cleansed man and let the living bird fly free.

Jesus was "delivered (to death) for our offences and raised again for our justification". It took two birds to represent how Jesus makes us clean. The bird that was dipped in the blood of the sacrificed bird was set free. The dead bird represented the sacrifice of Jesus delivered unto death on the cross and the released bird represented the resurrected Lord, our justification.

Then the leper washed himself in water and brought all the offerings of the law. His head, hand and foot were to be sprinkled with the blood of the Trespass offering and then anointed with oil on the right ear, thumb and toe.

The right is our best and foremost. The ear means we give our ear to the Spirit. Our hand is our service, to be directed by the Spirit, and our foot our direction in life. Everyone is either a leper or a cleansed leper. Which are you?

<u>The Blood</u>
The whole book of Leviticus gives great emphasis on blood sacrifice and the importance of blood. The life of the flesh is in the blood. Let us take a look at the meaning of the blood of Christ to us:
(Taken from *Christ in All the Scriptures*)

The meaning of the blood – Leviticus 17:11,14
Redemption through the blood – 1Peter 1:18,19
Forgiveness through the blood – Ephesians 1:7
Justification through the blood – Romans 5:9

Peace through the blood – Colossians 1:20
Cleansing through the blood – 1 John 1:7
Loosing from sin through the blood – Revelation 1:5
Enter the Holy Place by the blood – Hebrews 10:19
Victory through the blood - Revelation 12:11
Glory everlasting through the blood – Revelation 7:14,15

Does the precious blood of Christ mean all this to you? Pouring out His blood was pouring out His life so that all these things could be yours. That was the joy set before Him that gave Him the perseverance to go through the crucifixion. (Hebrews 12:2) Let the investment of His blood for you produce all the fruits for which He poured it out.

Jesus in Numbers

The book of Numbers tells us of the tragic account of the failure to enter the Promised Land. God in His grace and mercy had allowed the Israelites to take two years so that they would be prepared to enter and prepared to trust God for the battles ahead. (Exodus 13:17) But upon hearing the reports of 10 of the 12 spies, that the enemy was too powerful, they lost heart.

God's judgment on their rebellion against and lack of faith in the One who had sheltered and visibly guided them the last two years was to have them die in the desert. It was a very just judgment as it was one they had themselves chosen. (Numbers 14:2-3) Verse 3 is a clear declaration that they doubted the very heart of God in spite of all the illustrations and patience He had shown them. Be very careful of the options you give God. Watch the words that slip from your lips. The Israelites were not as different from us as you might think. Remember, Egypt is a picture of the world. Read 1Corinthians 10:1-6.

Is this a picture of the delivered Children of God today as God leads us to a life of victory and yet we refuse to trust Him and step into that life? Just like the Children of Israel were led to that border at the time when they were ready to enter, so God's Spirit leads us to a border that we must cross, believing that He can do what looks impossible to us. Don't doubt the heart of God and spend the rest of your life in the wilderness. Refuse to accept death in the desert as a substitute for entering into His rest!

Jesus in the Old Testament

Here is a display of the wonderful patience and mercy of God. The cloud still guided them and protected these doubting rebels from the sun. Their clothes still did not wear out. The manna still fell from above. Water still came from the Rock. *If we are faithless He remains faithful.* (2Timothy 2:13) He walks with us and provides for us even when we are being judged for our lack of faith in Him. Blessing isn't necessarily a sign you are in God's will. It just means that God is faithful.

The Cloud

The cloud stayed over the tabernacle and probably mushroomed out over the whole camp, shading them from the intense desert sun. Not only was it their guidance but it was their shelter. (Numbers 9:15) By night it was a pillar of fire giving light to the whole camp. What a night light! *He that followeth me shall not walk in darkness but shall have the light of life.* (John 8:12 KJV) It remained in place for a day or two or even a year and would move when they were meant to move.

The cloud was a Theophany of the Lord. (Exodus 13:21) He is our shelter through life, our light in the darkness. He is our guide. We must keep looking unto Jesus. When He moves we are to follow. Silver trumpets were used to announce the moving of the Cloud.

Silver Trumpets

Not only did silver trumpets announce time to break camp, but they called the men to war, and announced the feasts. Wherever one was in the camp, they could hear the call of the trumpets. *My sheep hear my voice and I know them and they follow me."*

(John 10:27) We should be listening for the voice of Jesus within our hearts as He announces the times to move, the times to go to battle in prayer, and the times to celebrate His goodness in our lives. The trumpets gave a clear call. Trust God to be able to speak to you clearly about your direction in life. God had no problem speaking to Moses. If you are willing to hear, He can clearly and easily speak to you.

Aaron
We have considered Aaron as the High Priest and the shadow he was of the Great High Priest to come. Numbers gives us another picture we have not seen yet. Just after the people were ready to stone Moses and Aaron for leading them to this land of giant enemies, the Lord sent a plague that swept through the camp. Aaron ran with his censor of incense to stand in front of the plague and stop its advancement.

What a picture of our Lord who was so verbally abused, and yet, went to stand before the sweeping deadly plague of sin so that we could live.
(Numbers 16:46-50) The censor is a picture of the prayers of Jesus to the Father on our behalf as He ever lives to make intercession. (Hebrews 7:25) Right now, He stands between you and the wages of sin, which is death, and intercedes for you to the Father.

It is incredible to me that only a short while later they questioned Moses choice of Aaron as a High Priest. See Numbers 17. They didn't mind letting him have the best of the tithe since he was not going to inherit any land, but now that the inheritance is 38 years away others wanted his title and role.

The rods of each tribal leader were placed before the Lord. The next morning, Aaron's rod, the symbol of his leadership and authority, had blossomed and had almonds on it. It was a dead stick, but it came to life and bore fruit. This was an early picture of the resurrection of Jesus. Resurrection is a sign that He alone is the Great High Priest, the chosen of God.

In the end-time the False Prophet will give resurrected life to the Antichrist in an attempt to claim this role. The difference is in the fruit.
(Matthew 7:20; Ephesians 5:9) Even when we witness the miraculous, we must discern by the fruit.

<u>The Water of Separation</u>
In Numbers 19, the water of separation was prescribed for those contaminated by touching death. The water was mixed with the ashes of a red heifer. This looks forward to the cleansing blood of Jesus. (1John 1:7) Perhaps this is the water Jesus was referring to when He told Nicodemus He had to be born of water and the Spirit, not the shadow but the reality of His blood.

<u>The Brazen Serpent</u>
In Numbers 21:4-9, the people again complained about their difficulties. As a judgment, fiery serpents were sent into the camp whose poisonous bite would bring a painful death. It is reported today that in this same area there are large snakes with fiery red dots and a poisonous bite. When the people confessed their sin, the Lord had Moses make a bronze serpent and put it on a pole. They had but to "look upon it and live". In John 3:14-15, Jesus claimed this to be a shadow of His coming death on the cross.

Bronze is a symbol of judgment. The pole pictures the cross. There on the cross is the image of what was bringing a painful death to the people, the serpent. *He hath made Him to be sin for us, who knew no sin: that we might be made the righteousness of God in Him.* (2Corinthians 5:21) Those people who were bitten had death in them. When they looked, they were not just healed of the puncture wounds, but they received life.

When Nicodemus puzzled over Jesus' expression of being born again, the Lord pointed him to this picture of new life. Jesus was declaring that everyone has been bitten by the poison of sin that brings death. He was going to be lifted up on a pole so that by looking to Him, we can live.

Take a look at the following pictures and see what you think. Are they valid pictures of Christ?

Prophecy of the Star
Compare Numbers 24:17,19 with Matthew 2:2 and Revelation 22:16

Moses Prayer
Numbers 27:16,17 Was this ultimately answered in Jesus Christ? Of course, Joshua was a fulfillment, but remember, Joshua is the same name as Jesus, Yeshua. He is God's chosen man. He is God's chosen priest. He is God's chosen Shepherd. Isn't that what Moses was truly seeking?

Just as God took Abraham's words about God providing a lamb, and made them come to pass in a way that Abraham could not imagine, so God took this prayer of Moses and did more than he could ask or imagine.

Jesus in Deuteronomy

Deuteronomy is a review of the life of Moses as he recounted the journeys and laws to his people just before he was to die. 'Obedience' could be called the keynote of the book. He would one day stand with Elijah and Christ on the mount of transfiguration and discuss Christ's obedience to the Father and ultimate destination of the cross in Jerusalem. But God's desire for obedience is always for the good of the people. See Deuteronomy 5:29 and 6:24. Obedience is not required to gain God's favor. It is expected because we already enjoy God's favor.

They were chosen, delivered, and heirs of wonderful promises. It is because the requests for obedience came from this heart of love that they are expected to obey. (Titus 2:12-14) We should be zealous to do good works, because His gift of grace has enabled us to obey the commands that are for our good.

Surrender
As they stood in the plains of Moab listening to Moses remind them of the Law, they pledged their obedience to God. (Deuteronomy 26:16-19) Today, too, we must come to a point of surrender when we decide we will obey Christ because of our love for Him and trust that He knows what is best for us. It is like the servant in Deuteronomy 15:16-17. *[16] But if your servant says to you, "I do not want to leave you," because he loves you and your family and is well off with you, [17] then take an awl and push it through his ear lobe into the door, and he will become your servant for life. Do the same for your maidservant.*

He had to come to a decision point of whether or not he loved his master enough to give up his life for him. Are you better off serving Jesus? Some of the servants of the Lord realize by a revelation of grace that they are better off as His slaves than a slave of our own desires. (Romans 6:16-18) Surrender to Jesus is in your best interest, just as it was in the best interest of the Jews to surrender to the Law and seen as true freedom.

The Promised Messiah
We learned in the study of Exodus that Moses was a type of Christ. (Deuteronomy 18:15) Let us just review a few of the shadows and also consider some of the ways the picture falls short. Delivered from a violent death at infancy, willing to leave the palace of a king to deliver his people from bondage, meekness, faithfulness, and in finishing the work God gave him to do, Moses was like Christ. Also, he was a mediator between God and the people, and communed with God face to face. Quite a likeness!

Yet here are some places the type falls short. *Moses was faithful in all God's house as a servant, but Christ as a Son over His own house."* (Hebrews 3:5-6 KJV) Moses sinned under provocation. Moses needed help to bear the burden of the people. Christ has borne the burden of our sins in His own body on the tree and invites us to cast all our care on Him. Moses was not able to bring the people into the Promised Land, but Christ is able to bring us in and give us an inheritance among all them that are sanctified by faith that is in Him. (Acts 20:32)

Cities of Refuge
See Deuteronomy 4:41-42. There were three cities of refuge on each side of the Jordan. They were chosen for their easy

access from any location. Roads to these cities were clearly marked. The gates were always open. If someone accidentally killed someone, he could flee to a city of refuge to be safe from the vengeance of a kinsman of the dead.

We also have a place of refuge in Jesus. Although Satan is out to punish us with death for our sins, we have fled to Jesus and are safe there in Him. Tradition says there were men standing on the highways who could direct you to the city, running before you to show the way. What a picture of an evangelist! (Romans 10:15)

The Cross
See Deuteronomy 21:23. This is a picture of the curse Jesus would take upon Himself along with that of all mankind as He hung on the cross for us.
(John 19:31; Galatians 3:13)

Blessings for Obedience
Deuteronomy 28 lists all the blessings for obedience. They are all ours in Christ Jesus. In Him we have the righteousness of God. (Ephesians 1:3) Not only that, but we are freed from all the curses of our past disobedience. (Galatians 3:13)

Circumcision of the Heart
Moses talked of the circumcision of the heart. See Deuteronomy 10:16 and 30:6. Compare those passages with Romans 2:28-29 and Colossians 2:11.

Life and Death
Moses set life and death before them. See Deuteronomy 30:15. *He that has the Son has life. He that has not the Son*

shall not see life, but the wrath of God abides on him. (John 3:36)

Word as Life
Moses said the Word was life in Deuteronomy 32:47. Jesus said the words He spoke are Spirit and life. John 6:63

The Urim and Thummim
The High Priest had the Urim and Thummim upon his breastplate and inquired of the Lord through them. We do not know exactly what they were, although it is speculated that they were stones of some type. We don't know how God answered through them. We do know that the Septuagint translated these words as 'manifestation' and 'truth'. Christ is the manifestation of the truth. We learn God's will as we behold Him.

About Benjamin Jacob prophesied: *Let the beloved of the LORD rest secure in him, for he shields him all day long, and the one the LORD loves rests between his shoulders.* (Deuteronomy 33:12) Is this not a picture of the Good Shepherd carrying his sheep? Also see verse 27.

This was a short chapter, so let's add a Christophany from the book of Joshua that is quite amazing.

[13] *Now when Joshua was near Jericho, he looked up and saw a man standing in front of him with a drawn sword in his hand. Joshua went up to him and asked, "Are you for us or for our enemies?"* [14] *"Neither," he replied, "but as commander of the army of the LORD I have now come." Then Joshua fell facedown to the ground in reverence, and asked him, "What message does my Lord have for his servant?"* [15] *The commander of the LORD's army replied,*

"Take off your sandals, for the place where you are standing is holy." And Joshua did so. (Joshua 5:13-15)

It sounds like Moses' experience with the burning bush, which must have been told to Joshua many times. Notice the prostrate reverence and the holy ground. (Revelation 19:10)

This is a Christophany, a preincarnate appearance of Jesus Christ. In Joshua 6:2 (KJV) the captain is called JHWH. Joshua needed his own encounter with God and so do we. The Captain of the Hosts gave Joshua his battle plan in chapter 6. We need to hear from the Captain to know how to gain victory over the enemy in our lives.

Jesus in the Old Testament

We finished looking at Jesus in the Pentateuch and we are now going to take a look at a few of the chief pictures of Jesus in the rest of the Old Testament. We touched on Joshua before, but let's consider him again since he has the same name as our Savior.

First, his assignment is to lead the Children of Israel into the Promised Land. In Hebrews 4:1-11 we learn that our Savior does what Joshua did but in a more ultimate spiritual sense. He leads us in victory over our enemies, gives us homes we did not build, and leads us into a place of abundance.

Joshua was told no man could stand against him (Joshua 1:5), just as no man could stand against our Savior. He was told that the LORD would be with him as He was with Moses, that is, face to face. He would go in and come out, meeting with God for the people. That is what our Savior does.

Joshua is a man that leads an army against the enemies of Jehovah. That reminds us of the title Lord of Hosts, who is none other than Jesus. We have no record of blemish in Joshua's character. Though it is certain that he sinned, none is recorded.

<u>The Judges</u>
Judges follows Joshua, and in the sense that they are all deliverers against an oppressor, they are all a type of the great Deliverer or Savior. Jesus personally appears three times in Judges, 2:1f, 6:11f, 13:1f especially 13:18. Take a look.

Jesus Concealed in the Old Testament

In the book of Ruth we have the Kinsman Redeemer, Boaz. In Boaz, whose name means 'ability', we see our Redeemer Who purchased the church to be His bride. Look at Ruth 4:4-12. Man lost the title of the earth (property) to Satan in the Garden. Only man could gain the title back, redeeming the land. Since no man could because of sin, (Psalm 49:7-9) God became man. He is our kinsman, but being sinless, He is *able* to redeem. When He did so He also took us as His bride, purchasing us with His own blood. (Acts 20:28)

Samuel

Sumu was a common word to ancient Hebrews and in Babylonian meant 'son'. When Hannah's prayer was answered, she kept her part of the bargain and gave him to the Lord, even naming him Sumu El, son of God. Do you think perhaps he could be a type of the Son of God? Hannah and Mary sang similar songs and both had the same vision. Compare 1Samuel 2:10 with Luke 1:51-55. Hannah is the first in Scripture to use the name *Messiah,* and her song and the name of her son are prophetic of Christ.

Samuel combined the offices of prophet, priest, and ruler just as our Lord does. The *Schools of the Prophets* that he established remind us of the outpouring of the Spirit with the gifts of apostles, evangelists and teachers.

But most of all, Samuel was a picture of Jesus in his prayer life and intercession. God lists him with Moses as a great intercessor in Jeremiah 15:1. See his heart in 1Samuel 12:23. He started his communion with God as a child. Samuel was respected, loved and feared. He had quite a resemblance to Jesus, who he foreshadowed. I think he spent so much time with Him that he began to look like Him. If that is true, shouldn't we be doing the same?

David

Outside the Pentateuch, David is probably the clearest type of Christ. The similarities begin with their births in Bethlehem. It continues with the knowledge of the call at an early age, Jesus on the temple visit, and David upon Samuel's visit. Then, with the quiet years, David watching the flocks and Jesus in His earthly father's carpentry shop. David risked his life for the sheep fighting a lion and a bear. Jesus gave His life for the sheep fighting a lion that walks about seeking whom he may devour.

In giving His life, He was victorious like David. The Shepherd and King were blended in David and in David's Son.

It is interesting to note these parallels:
The Good Shepherd in death – John 10:11, Psalm 22
The Great Shepherd in resurrection – Hebrews 13:20, Psalm 23
The Chief Shepherd in glory – 1 Peter 5:4, Psalm 24

David was anointed three times, first in his father's house, once over Judah, and finally over Israel. God has anointed Jesus with the oil of gladness, as King of kings, and Lord of Lords. Just as David was anointed and remained in exile while another ruled, so Jesus waits while this world's prince's reign comes to an end. When David was anointed king in Hebron (2Samuel 2:4), "*The Spirit clothed Amasai and he said, 'Thine are we, David, and on thy side.'*" (1Chronicles 12:18 KJV) That sounds like our own recognition of Christ as King within our hearts as the Kingdom comes to us. Someday we will look in His face and declare, "*Thou art my King.*" (Psalm 44:4 KJV)

(Deuteronomy 17:15; Hebrews 2:17) We never read of David being defeated and this pictures our victorious Lord over our enemy, Satan. (Isaiah 9:7)

David took the stronghold of Zion. This is like the fortress of our will. Once that is surrendered to the Lord, His reign is established.

<u>Mephibosheth</u> is a picture of the grace of our King. Even though we are crippled and were of the household of the one who sought His life, He brings us into His own household and makes us as one of the King's sons, dining at His table continually. And what is it that is laid upon the table? It is His life that is food for all who will come. *The bread that I give is my flesh.* (John 6:51 KJV)

Then, Absalom is sent into exile for the murder of his brother. David's mourning for him reminds us of God's love for the lost. *The King… wept very sore… And David mourned for his son every day…And the soul of David longed to go forth unto Absalom.*
(2Samuel 13:36-39 KJV) But then hear the words of the woman of Tekoa, *God deviseth means, that he that is banished be not an outcast from Him* (2Samuel 14:14 RV) This reminds us of God's plan to redeem the lost.

But Absalom still rebelled and tried to establish himself as king. Even in the midst of rebellion against David's love and generosity, David still asked his soldiers to deal gently with him and wished he could give his life in Absalom's place. That is the heart of Jesus for you!

As David left Jerusalem, the same way Jesus entered for the last time, a group of 600 Philistines led by Ittai from Gath joined him. They must have been won over by his integrity and anointing when he was in hiding from Saul in Ziklag. As they came to the Kidron, which was flooding, David pleaded with them to return, and warned that they might be joining a lost cause.

Ittai and company would not leave his side and passed over with their families to follow David into a second exile. Whether in life or death, he would not leave his master's side. When David wanted to join them in battle, they refused to let him, telling him that he was worth ten thousand of them.

When Jesus went over the same brook and climbed the same Mount of Olives, He did not have a huge band of soldiers. Only 11 men were with him, and they could not watch with him one hour. When the enemy came, they forsook the Fairest of 10,000. He laid down His life for those same deserters. Do we have the devotion of Ittai who would not leave his side even in disgrace and seeming defeat? We can still make His heart glad by standing with Him as the world scorns Him.

In Shemei, who cursed David, we have the scorners who mocked the Savior on the cross. In Ahithophel's advice to Absalom we have the similarity to our Lord, *"I will smite the King only"*. He was *"smitten and stricken of God"* for us.

The good news in this shadow is that upon the defeat of the rebels, King David crosses over the Jordan (a symbol of death) and returns to reign. Tradition says all Judah went out to meet him on the other side of the Jordan and bring him back. *The dead in Christ shall rise first, and then we that remain will be caught up to meet Him in the air.*

(1Thessalonians 4:16-17 KJV) He will return on a white horse with a sword blazing from His mouth, and the armies

of heaven will follow. (Revelation 19:11-16) There will be no challenge to His reign then.

See what David is promised by God in
1Chronicles 17:11-14 *When your days are over and you go to be with your fathers, I will raise up your offspring to succeed you, one of your own sons, and I will establish his kingdom. ^{12} He is the one who will build a house for me, and I will establish his throne forever. ^{13} I will be his father, and he will be my son. I will never take my love away from him, as I took it away from your predecessor. ^{14} I will set him over my house and my kingdom forever; his throne will be established forever.*

The only One who is alive today that can claim to be heir of this promise is Jesus Christ. Even so Lord Jesus, come quickly!

Jeremiah
He was known before his birth. He was set apart in the womb. He was a prophet to the nations. He was appointed to tear down and build up. He predicted the destruction of Jerusalem. (Jeremiah 22:5-7; Matthew 23:37-39) He wept. He was rejected by his people. (Jeremiah 26:7-11; John 1:11) He was imprisoned because of his preaching. He was tried for treason. (Jeremiah 11:18-23; 20:1-6; Mark 14:53-65) Predicted the New Covenant (Jeremiah 31:31-34) and the return of the Messiah. (Jeremiah 23:5-7; Matthew 24:27) Oh, did you think I was talking about Jeremiah. I was referring to Jesus.

Conclusion

This is the end of our study, but I hope it is not the end of your discovery of Jesus in the Old Testament. Would you consider for a moment the heart of God that gave us picture after picture and prophetic word on prophetic word about His Son? Is He trying to tell us something?

The message seems to be that everything is about Jesus. It is almost as if the Father could not wait to tell us about the Son, so He put pictures, types and shadows, throughout His story of His revelation to man. After all, the Bible is all about God revealing Himself to us, and we see Him most clearly in the Son.

Surely, He wanted us not be in doubt about who Jesus was when He arrived at that perfect moment in history. That is why He gave us so many pictures and prophecies. Perhaps it is also for a day to come in which the Jewish people will finally have the veil lifted and see Jesus throughout their sacred Torah scrolls.

The author of Hebrews tells us to fix our eyes upon Jesus. The Greek word he used means to turn away from other things to see something. (Hebrews 12:2) I trust that as you have pondered the grand design of God the Father, you have realized how important it is for us to fix our eyes upon our Savior. He is the manifest presence of God. He is the One we will worship forever.

If you have not surrendered to His rule in your life, you have missed the one thing God wants to get across to mankind.

Jesus is Lord. He has been given the title to all things. He will reign forever. We owe our life and our service to Him. Do you have anything that you did not receive from Him? (1Corinthians 4:7) The wonder is that He loves us.

He loves you so much that He died in your place that you might spend eternity with Him. Have you surrendered to that love? Is your life about Him, like the sacred Scriptures are about Him?

The Apostle Paul said that his purpose in living was that the life of Christ might be revealed in him. (2Corinthians 4:10-11) You see, just as the Father revealed Jesus in the Scriptures, He wants your life to reveal His Son as well. It begins when you ask Him to be the Lord (master) of your life. You must turn your thinking around and take on the mind of Christ. Peter declared that those who repent (have a mind revolution) and are baptized (representing a death to your old ways and rising to new life) would receive the promised Holy Spirit. (Acts 2:38) The baptism of the Spirit, the lordship of Christ or full surrender, I don't care what you call it, it's the presence and power of God in your life to represent Jesus to the world you come in contact with. Then it can be said that Jesus is revealed in you.

Just as this book is entitled, Jesus Concealed in the Old Testament, we can say Jesus concealed in those who receive Him and surrender to His reign in their hearts. The things you do and say at the leading of His Spirit within you will be a picture to all of the grace and love of Jesus. What a privilege! What an assignment! There is no higher calling.

During Jesus' last week the Greeks came to Philip and said, *"Sir, we would like to see Jesus."... ^{23} Jesus replied, "The* *hour has come for the Son of Man to be glorified. ²⁴ I tell you the truth, unless a kernel of wheat falls to the ground and dies, it remains only a single seed. But if it dies, it produces many seeds. ²⁵ The man who loves his life will lose it, while the man who hates his life in this world will keep it for eternal life. ²⁶ Whoever serves me must follow me; and where I am, my servant also will be. My Father will honor the one who serves me."* (John 12:23-26)

What a strange answer! Yet, if you understand Jesus' desire to be revealed through you to the seeking world, it makes perfect sense. He could not physically go to all that were seeking Him. When the world began to seek Him, it was time for the seed to be planted. Now it is time for you and me to go to those who would see Jesus.

Let others see Jesus in me! *For me to live is Christ...* (Philippians 1:21) If you will live a life of surrender to the Spirit of God, the desire of God to reveal Jesus to the world will come to fulfillment through your life. Your words and actions at the direction of the Spirit will reveal Christ to the world. Then what is true of the Old Testament will be true in your life as well; Jesus will be seen by a seeking world.

A life for self, no matter how great in the eyes of the world, is of no significance in eternity. But a life lived in revealing Jesus to the world not only pleases the heart of God but has a great affect on the eternal souls of many.
²⁶ What good will it be for a man if he gains the whole world, yet forfeits his soul? Or what can a man give in exchange for his soul? ²⁷ For the Son of Man is going to come in his Father's glory with his angels, and then he will reward each person according to what he has done. (Matthew 16:26-27)

These are the words of the One we have been reading about. Just as the past faithfully predicted His first coming, you can count on the words of Jesus about His Second Coming to be just as dependable. When He comes will you be rewarded for the way you revealed Christ to a spiritually starving world? Will you live to manifest Christ in your mortal body?

^{10} We always carry around in our body the death of Jesus, so that the life of Jesus may also be revealed in our body. ^{11} For we who are alive are always being given over to death for Jesus' sake, so that his life may be revealed in our mortal body.
(2Corinthians 4:10-11)

Conclusion